A CHILD FROM "THE BOROUGH"

To. Jenny. Bill. & Family.
with all good wishes for your
long and happy friendship.
from. Catherine. July 1992.

A CHILD FROM "THE BOROUGH"

Catherine Down

ARTHUR H. STOCKWELL LTD.
Elms Court   Ilfracombe   Devon
Established 1898

© *Catherine Down, 1992*
First published in Great Britain, 1992

All rights reserved.
No part of this publication may be reproduced
or transmitted in any form or by any means,
electronic or mechanical, including photocopy,
recording, or any information storage and
retrieval system, without permission
in writing from the copyright holder.

ISBN 0 7223 2638-6
*Printed in Great Britain by
Arthur H. Stockwell Ltd.
Elms Court   Ilfracombe
Devon*

CONTENTS

List of Illustrations		6
Preface		7
Part One — 1910—1926		9
Part Two — 1926—1936		20
Part Three — 1936—1944		26
Part Four — 1944—1952		35
Part Five — 1952—1955		41
Part Six — 1955—1970		67
Part Seven		73

ILLUSTRATIONS

Frontispiece: Southwark Cathedral. (Reproduced by kind permission of Southwark Arts, Libraries and Entertainments, Local Studies Library).

Set between pp.32—33

Our sports group, Shirley Schools, Croydon, Surrey 1921. With Mr Roberts, Headmaster; Miss Capes, Matron; Mr Small, Sports Master. Competing against Addiscombe Girls School, Shirley winning the Shield. Myself in the centre holding it.

Myself sitting in an ornamental alcove of our Nurses' Home, 1937.

In a friend's garden at Carshalton beeches with "Bimbo", one of the hospital kittens who needed a good home.

Prize Giving Day at the West Norfolk & Kings Lynn Hospital, 1942. Doctors, Matron and nursing staff, with a representative from the Royal College of Nursing.

At Flete Maternity Unit, Lord Mildmay's Estate 1944—1946, for the benefit of the Press. We were only pretending to be picking the daffodils!

Albion Street House, Kingston-upon-Hull, East Yorkshire (now known as North Humberside). Part Two Training School for Midwives, 1948.

My brother, James Down. Taken just before the 1939—1945 war. He was a Corporal in the Middlesex Regiment and died on active service, April 1943. His name is on the Memorial Roll of Honour.

PREFACE

This is a true account of my life as I remember it. Finding out who I really was after leaving school, by being given my birth certificate, when I was fifteen years of age.

I knew September was the month of my birth, but never the actual date.

Then always being called Kitty or Katie, I discovered my one and only Christian name to be Catherine, which I thought was very nice, and so I always used it after escaping from the fetters of domestic service into a life of freedom, determined to live my life as I felt sure God was planning for me.

I have since proved that when one door closed another has opened, leading me throughout to a very interesting and satisfying life, able to enjoy his beautiful world, both in my leisure and in my working life. *"Mostly as a Midwife"*. Never ceasing to marvel at God's most wonderful and perfect handiwork. *God's creation of Mankind.*

C. Down

PART ONE   1910—1926

As a stone gathers moss, in the woods by a rill,
So we fashion our lives, for good, or for ill,
By a thought, a word, a deed, or a smile,
As I live my life Lord, make it worthwhile.
Anon

I was born in London, "Charles Dickens' London", the area known as "The Borough", quite near Southwark Cathedral. It was September and somehow I imagine it to have been a lovely late summer's day; trees all still in their summer glory, the sun's rays penetrating their branches, with the birds sharing their leafy boughs. It's much quieter now, having brought up their families and preparing them for the great task of migration to warmer climes, as the colder days are approaching. My life in some ways portrays that of a brood. The last of the family — four boys, four girls; but because of circumstances beyond our control, we never knew each other. The Great War 1914—1918 was looming. Father was called up for active service, as were my two older brothers, and all died serving their country. Mother, left to cope with such a family, could no longer do justice to their welfare on little money, so it seems four of the children went into Local Authority Cottage Homes in Surrey, administered by the London County Council. I, being the youngest, followed after a period in a Children's Nursery, between the age of two and three years. My memory goes way back to those days. I remember clearly climbing onto a table and falling over a big fire-guard, ending up inside it, burning the back of my head.

I have the scar to this day.

The time arrived when I too went to live in the same Homes as the rest of the family, but we never had an opportunity of meeting as we were all in different cottages. Not even, when each one left school, did we know when, or where, they went. That I think was the tragedy of our family's separation. "The Homes" were in lovely grounds near Shirley village, Croydon. There was a large school building, a swimming-pool, and laundry block. Our School Hall was used for choir practice. We always had a very good choir where we performed on our Annual Sports day, held during the summer months. Our cottages were built in blocks of two, detached. All had lovely small gardens with stretches of grass to front and rear. On our side was an enclosed apple orchard, and lots of lovely trees. There was what we called a Boys and a Girls side, quite separate, so we never met with the boys, not even during school hours. The cottages were all named after trees, shrubs and flowers. Mine was "Holly", next door, "Heather". It was here, in my young days, that I first learnt to love the countryside — gardens, flowers and animals — although we only had a cat, a beautiful black and white Persian, called Whisky, whom I adored; Whisky providing the only really good laugh I had during my school days. One lovely summer's day with all the cottage doors open, he rushed in from the garden, flew along the passage in one of his joyous moods and, finding the parlour door open, took a flying leap onto the table in the middle of the room, where there was a large aspidistra in a fancy china pot on a table-cloth covering a polished table. Could you imagine the chaos, when Whisky, table-cloth and aspidistra, all landed on the floor with an almighty crash! The plant and pot broken into smithereens?

Whisky vanished the way he came. Unhurt. I could see the funny side of this episode and had a good laugh. Though it wasn't quite so funny when I had to help clear up the mess!

Our Homes each housed fourteen children. There was a House Mother in each, mostly middle-aged, maiden ladies. My first House Mother who must have retired when I was about nine years of age was very kind. When I first arrived I was the youngest in the cottage, and was very happy. I remember being given a lovely strawberry-pink dress and white lace socks as best apparel for Sundays. Then when Miss Shaw retired I was very sad, as our next House Mother was very much her opposite. Meting out punishment chores, which were most unpleasant at times and very often not knowing what we had done to deserve them. Well do I remember one winter's evening after a pouring wet day I was given the task of cleaning all the children's boots. We never had shoes. The boots were handed down from one child to another as they grew out of them. I had to clean these boots in an outhouse without any lights, and because they were so wet could not get a shine on them. When I had taken them in for inspection I was told to take them out and do them all again. My remark was that I could not see. House Mother's reply was, "If you cannot see, you can feel". I went to bed very unhappy that night.

Our day began at 6 a.m. when a very loud hooter, from a central point, roared out all over the Homes. Then it was all go until bedtime. Breakfast was about 7 a.m., consisting always of bread and dripping and cocoa. When we were old enough we all had work to do before we went to school and before we returned from lunch, always called dinner in those days, and again after tea in the evening.

In our cottage kitchen there was a big black range (stove) heated by coal which supplied all the hot water and where all the food was cooked. We in turn had the job of keeping it clean with blacklead and brushes. The large fender surround together with huge tongs and shovel were of steel, which were cleaned with emery paper until they shone like silver. It was hard but rewarding work. Our cottage was the furthest away from the school building so we had to run all the way back to dinner and when school was over for the day, for fear of being late when we would get extra work to do.

I really enjoyed going to school and liked school work with the different teachers. One, a nice young lady with lovely auburn hair, a Miss Hampton, returned as a Mrs Boot after one of the school's vacations. She was a member of the Croydon Amateur Dramatic Society. Then there was an elderly teacher, a Miss Blythe, who always wore black stockings, which she would bring to school to have mended.

She would ask for a volunteer to darn them. This particular day no one was forthcoming so I put up my hand. "Thank you", said Miss Blythe, "one volunteer is worth ten pressed men". If I remember rightly that was not the last time I got the job. Mr Wright, my third teacher, was kind and helpful and kept our minds active. About that time the wireless was being invented. "Crystal sets". We were allowed to help with the making of them, winding the coils of wire onto the parts that went inside the casings, and being told and instructed about the most important part, namely the "cat's whisker". I only once got the cane from a lady teacher. She had been giving us a lesson on how a pearl was formed inside an oyster shell, producing a secretion to cover a foreign body, such as a piece of sand or grit which was causing some irritation. I was intrigued and took in every detail. The next day we were asked to write a composition on the previous day's lesson. I was quite excited and wrote what I thought would make a good story. Alas, in my enthusiasm I left out all the full stops and commas, so I was in dead trouble and got the cane, which did more damage psychologically than physically. I always looked forward to the poetry lessons which I suppose were really introduced during my primary school days. Our nature study lessons were mostly by verse. For instance:—

The River from its Source

Oh tell me pretty river,
Whence do thy waters flow,
And whither art thou roaming,
So pensive and so slow.

My birthplace was the mountain,
My nurse the April showers,
My cradle was a fountain,
All curtained by wild flowers.

One morn I ran away,
A madcap hoyden rill,
And many a prank that
Day I played, adown the hill.

> And then mid meadowy banks,
> I flirted with the flowers,
> That stooped with glowing lips,
> To woo me to their bowers.
>
> But these bright scenes are o'er,
> And darkly flows my way,
> I hear the ocean roar,
> And there must be my grave.

I have no idea who wrote *The River*. I never kept a diary, but have always remembered them. Somehow, I always got caught up in the atmosphere of the places that the following were written about.

Alfred Tennyson's	The Lady of Shallot. Morte D'Arthur.
Longfellow's	Hiawatha and his lovely wife, Minnie Ha Ha (Laughing Water), in that wonderful wilderness of ice and snow.

> Oh! the long and dreary winter,
> Oh! the cold and cruel winter,
> Even thicker, thicker, thicker,
> Froze the ice, on lake and river.
> Ever deeper, deeper, deeper,
> Fell the snow, o'er all the landscape.

Gray's	Elergy. Written in Stoke Poges Churchyard in Buckinghamshire. All thirty-two verses of it. The property now owned by The National Trust.
Shakespeare's	The Seven Stages of Man, and many others.
Thomas Moore's	"The Meeting of the Waters" in the Vale of Avoca, in beautiful County Wicklow, Ireland.
Coleridge's	The Ancient Mariner.
Wordsworth's	With his Hosts of Golden Daffodils,

to name but a few. Over the years they have remained in my memory and in adult life I have visited almost all the places associated with them.

Our swimming-pool, where we were all taught to swim, was great fun for most of the children, but any who hesitated got pushed into the shallow end; so we all soon learnt. One little girl, no more than four years old, who lived in the cottage next door, loved it and could swim like a fish. I often wondered what happened to her, she was younger than me.

It was really sad that we never had the opportunity of making friends. Not even with our own brothers and sisters, as I have already mentioned. I do just remember seeing my brother James, who was two and a half years older than me. He lived at Willow Cottage and his House Mother and my first House Mother were friends. Mine was an expert at making Christmas cakes and decorated them beautifully with marzipan and icing sugar, and always made one for Willow Cottage. So on this particular Christmas Day afternoon we walked to Willow Cottage and had tea there. That was the only time I saw my brother at school, for when he was fifteen he left. I never knew when or where he went, but got to know later that he was sent into the Merchant Navy.

I cannot remember much about our Christmases, only that every child had a newly-minted silver sixpenny piece on Christmas Day, and that was our pocket-money for the year. I always associate oranges with Christmas, because that was the only time we saw them.

During the war we were restricted as to where we could go and I was eight years old when it ended. We were fortunate indeed that we did not suffer the hardships that other children may have done in their own homes. Even though I had been deprived of the love of a family I have always been grateful that I was able to live in such a nice place, in beautiful surroundings. We were well looked after in nice warm conditions, with good food, and enough of it.

I can remember quite a few things that happened during the war. The terrible explosion one evening at the ammunition factory at Silvertown, London. The noise could be heard miles away. Then on late summer afternoons going out into the fields to gather buckets full of acorns for the pigs. Oh! how I loved that. One day a girl at school told me that an aircraft had made a false landing in a field behind her cottage, so I asked her if she would take me to see it. How we managed it I don't exactly know, but we did go, just the two of us. It was the first aircraft I had ever seen. It may have been a small Handley-Page which was damaged on one side, having hit a hedge on landing. Part of the passenger side had been torn away, clearly showing the inside, with just room enough for one wicker armchair. I do not think anyone was hurt, as the rest of the plane was intact.

Then of course, no one who remembers the 1918 influenza epidemic, could ever forget it. So many people died. All the children in our cottage had it, including myself. We were all nursed in the cottage as our hospital was full. Thankfully we all recovered.

And so the war came to an end and things took on a more normal attitude. We were at last able to go outside our school gates on walks with our House Mother, on Saturday afternoons and during school holidays. We were brought up Church of England and attended St. John's Church in Shirley village. At the age of thirteen or fourteen we had to be confirmed, but understood little of what it really meant, remembering far more clearly the instructions called out in church, "Keep your feet off the hassocks". "Don't make so much noise when you kneel", and "What is a parable?", repeating like a lot of parrots, "An earthly story with a heavenly meaning". I never ever remembered hearing the Gospels preached. Yet I knew in my heart that I would soon learn to love the Christian faith. It was the only thing I had to cling to if I was to make anything out of my life.

Our vicar was a very elderly gentleman, who rarely preached as there was a younger one appointed. However, Reverend Wilkes did take the services occasionally. His voice was weak and he wore a wig, but I liked listening to him. Reverend Wilkes lived in the vicarage across the road which was named "The Wilderness". The garden was left to go its own way but that was how he liked it. There were a lot of crab-apple trees in his garden, and we were allowed to pick them when ripe. They made lovely crab-apple jelly. At the back of the church there was a large field where often two donkeys would be grazing, so on our way to Shirley Hills we would try to take them a carrot. Reverend Wilkes was a great nature lover and I have always understood that it was he who founded the Shirley Poppy from the wild ones that grew in the fields behind the church. I like to think that this was so, but have since heard it disputed that it was Shirley, Southampton. Shirley, Surrey was such a small place, that few people would have known of its existence.

On our way to church we had to go past a row of wooden cottages. They all had lovely pretty gardens. One cottage housed a big family named Rogers. They were lovely-looking children with curly hair and rosy complexions. One time when we were passing, one of the girls, about ten years old, had broken her leg and had it in plaster from the toes to her thigh. She was sitting in the baby's pram with her leg stretched out across it. Some of the family were having to push her all the way to Croydon General Hospital which was a good two miles or more. I did feel so sorry for the poor child and also the "pushers".

Often as we were waiting in the churchyard to go into the church my love of verse prompted me to read the inscriptions on some of the tombstones, and so learnt one or two by heart.

*A verse on an old tombstone
in Shirley Parish Church, Croydon (1924):*

Here rests his head upon this lap of earth.
A youth to fortune and to fame unknown,
Fair science frowned not on his humble birth,
But melancholy, marked him for her own.
Large was his bounty and his soul sincere,
Heaven did a recompense as largely send.
He gave to misery all he had, a tear.
He gained from Heaven, 'twas all he wished, "A Friend".

Our school holidays amounted to two weeks in the summer and two days at Easter, Whitsun and Christmas. Part of the summer vacation was taken up helping to clean the big school, scrubbing floors, steps, etc. We loved going to Shirley Hills with their stately pine-trees, sandy dunes, which centuries previously must have been submerged under the sea. The many paths running up and down and through the trees, fashioned by countless pairs of children's feet, who over the years had enjoyed their beauty and the freedom of such terrain. Sometimes we would even find an odd penny that had been dropped. There was also a disused "Smock Windmill" of 1855 in the grounds of Windmill House, owned by a wealthy family. The windmill is still there as an ancient monument and is now being restored. The new John Ruskin Grammar School has been built on the site and one has to obtain permission from the school's headmaster to view it. I was quite sad to see how much the whole area had changed, almost beyond recognition.

One holiday time we were looking forward to having an afternoon out on Shirley Hills and were probably discussing it after we went to bed. We were never allowed to talk after we went upstairs. The next day to our great disappointment our outing was cancelled because we had been talking in bed. For punishment we all, about six of us, had to sit along the wall of the wash-room floor turning sheets, sides to middle. This meant oversewing the selvage sides, then they were cut down the middle and hemmed on the other two sides. Normally this was only done when the sheets wore thin in the middle, to give them a longer life span. This particular day I think nearly-new sheets were cut in half, to keep us out of mischief. Our wash-room was a most uncomfortable place to sit in. It had a mosaic coloured stone floor, a row of wash-basins on one side and on the opposite wall a row of pegs where we hung our flannels and towels. They were all numbered. I was number six. We were very glad to see the end of that day.

I remember once going to Shirley Hills just in time to see a horse-drawn open-top bus arriving full of ladies out for the afternoon. There were no tarmacadam roads in those days, just dusty gravel roads. The ladies would not have had a very comfortable ride, but it was a sight well worth seeing.

One year some of us were taken to a service in Westminster Abbey, on Maundy Thursday, where her late Majesty Queen Mary, distributed the Maundy money to some of the elderly people of the district. Another time we went to the Crystal Palace, alas, no longer there. Also the Wembley Exhibition. Then another day I had an unexpected treat; the House

Mother next door was taking one of her girls out for the day to visit one of her relations. I think it may have been her mother, and she asked me if I would like to go. We took our lunch and had tea at the house. It was a cosy little terraced house and I remember there was a bowl of shrimps on the table for tea. I cannot remember whether I had any as I am allergic to any shellfish now, and dare not touch it. It was a most enjoyable day out for me and gave me an insight into what I had missed in life. I only ever saw my mother once when I was about seven years old. I went into a London hospital for a tonsillectomy and my mother came to see me there and stayed what I thought to be a very short time, leaving me a packet of sweets. I never saw or heard from my mother again. All I can think is that she always had to work, never having enough money for getting about. The war widows only had a few shillings a week in those days to live on.

I was born the year the Girl Guides' Association was founded. When I was old enough I joined the School Pack. Our Captain lived at West Wickham, not all that far from Shirley. One weekend we camped in an orchard at West Wickham and had a wonderful time. I think it must have been the tenth anniversary of the Guides' Association, for there was to be a big Guide Rally at St. Mary's Church, the Parish Church of Croydon. Six hundred Guides assembled from all the surrounding districts. It was a wonderful gathering. A beautiful service. Could you ever imagine anything more stirring than six hundred Guides all singing, "Onward Christian Soldiers"? A great experience, which made a lasting impression on me. The real highlight of our year was our annual Sports Day and exhibition of the children's work in our School Hall. As far as I can remember we always had a fine day. I enjoyed the different sports fixtures which we participated in outside in the fields, after which the School Choir sang their pieces and then the prizes were awarded. To my delight one year I had a prize for dressing a doll. It was a good size and had to be dressed in crochet work. I dressed her all in pink with bonnet, booties and a pretty patterned dress. I can see that doll now. My prize was a box of white cotton handkerchiefs with a coloured flower embroidered in the corner of each. I had never before seen anything as nice, let alone owned such a prize. I literally kept them for years in the box. They seemed too nice to use, but of course were eventually used long after my school days were over. I have always been a great sports fan and still am. We were encouraged to take an interest in it. One year our school competed against a school at Addiscombe, the next village on the Croydon side of Shirley where the open-top trams rattled down Cherry Orchard Road into George Street, past the old Alms Houses into Croydon High Street. We were delighted when our school won the Shield at the Addiscombe Sports. I have an old photograph of myself, the smallest, sitting in the middle of the front row holding the Shield.

The years all too quickly passed, and at fourteen I left the actual school work, having got into the top class. We then had our last year brushing up on our domestic working life, helping in the cottage. Doing a spell in the sewing-room where we were taught to use a treadle sewing-machine; we made night-dresses cut all in one piece, Magyar shape, and other garments for the children. Lastly, several weeks in the school laundry which I enjoyed the most. All the ladies that worked there lived in their own homes outside Shirley Schools, so there was less of an institutional atmosphere about the work. We felt we were one of a big family. They were all so kind and helpful.

With this being the last of my school career instructions, my school days regrettably came to an end. The unknown world outside Shirley School gates held no real feeling of joy for I was going into domestic service. My mistress, being one of our school committee members, and I the only servant in a three-storied house in London. So on the 6th day of March 1926, I was on my way, abruptly cut off from the companionship of other children. Nowhere to go, no garden, no pets, no friends, no Girl Guides, only work! Five months of real gloom, shedding many a tear. However, it turned out to be a stepping-stone to better worlds ahead. The family moved five months later to a nice house with a garden, to my favourite county, Surrey.

PART TWO   1926—1936

I will instruct thee and teach thee,
In the way that thou wilt go,
I will guide thee with mine eye.
                    Psalm 32—8

The family moved into their new home in the late summer of 1926. A three-bedroomed house with a box-room, large garden to the rear of the house, small front garden with a raised bank, in front of the lawn, which I eventually made into a rockery. Being virgin soil the whole garden needed to be planned and cultivated. My eyes feasted on the garden next door to the left of our house. It was absolutely beautiful. An elderly family lived there and must have been there quite a time to have got the garden into such prime condition. A blaze of colour nearly all the year round. My bedroom was the box-room, and my old lumpy flock mattress followed me from London. No matter how hard I shook and pummelled it about it remained most uncomfortable until the day I left eight years later. Yes, eight years of pure toleration, for I was unhappy at having to start my life in domestic service, having had to spend all my young days in that environment.

My sitting-room was the kitchen, when I had time to sit. However, having no home to go to and only an Elementary school education, which was not enough to convince anyone that I could do anything other than domestic work, I knew I would just have to bide my time, until I was old enough to work things out for myself. I hoped that my Faith, coupled with sheer determination and perseverance would eventually lead me along the right paths. Insidiously I began by reading the daily newspaper after the family had finished with it and bought the *Schoolgirls Own* magazine which was quickly replaced by the *Childrens Newspaper*, full of up-to-date and interesting information about what was going on in the world, though I must confess I did look forward to the cartoon of "Jacko" the Chimp. I had many a laugh to myself. He was always getting into all sorts of mischief.

I had very little money and not much time off to go anywhere. My day began before 7 a.m. and I was kept busy until bedtime. My first eighteen months went by with nothing unusual happening. But the next year, 1928, the family were going for a holiday during the summer so I was elated at the thought of getting away on my own. I had never seen the sea so made arrangements to go to Bournemouth and got accommodation in "The Christian Alliance", Women and Girls' Holiday Home. Everything was so cheap in those days. Five shillings return coach journey and full board for seventeen and sixpence for the week.

When I first stepped off the coach I stood glued to the promenade railings. It was a lovely sunny day as I stood taking in the wonderful expanse of sea, sky and coastline. My spending money was very limited, but found that not to matter, with God's beautiful creations to enjoy stretched out before my very eyes. Plenty of lovely walks through the parks. Branscombe Chine, the Beaches and promenade. It was all so different to what I had imagined. One evening I went for the first time in my life to the theatre in Bournemouth to see "The Good Companions"; the then young Jessie Matthews was performing there. My first holiday was soon over — I had enjoyed it immensely and vowed to myself that I would return the following year, which I did. Now that each year I had something to look forward to I went about my work with a much lighter tread.

After two holidays at Bournemouth, I decided to go somewhere different each year. The next one was to Worthing, Sussex. There again I stayed in a Christian Guest House, and met up with several girls who all went to the Baptist Church near where I was working. What a great time we had together. There were "The Children's Special Service

Missions" each day on the Beach. We all went, enjoying the singing and joining in the choruses, listening also to the Gospel messages which gave me much food for thought. I had never been to church since I left Shirley but plucked up courage after the holiday and asked if I could go to the Baptist Church on Sunday evenings. I then had every other Sunday evening off. Sometimes I would be invited out to one of the girl's homes to tea and then on to the 6 p.m. service.

The next year nearly all the girls that I had met at Worthing were planning a holiday to the Isle of Wight, where we stayed in the Girls' Friendly Society Hostel at Ryde. From there we had some lovely rambles through the country lanes around Whippingham, which I particularly liked. Lots of cottage gardens, gay with flowers, chickens running about free to enjoy their short lives. Another day we went to Seaview and rambled to Whytecliffe Bay where we enjoyed our packed lunch on the beach. Shanklin, Sandown, Ventnor, Cowes, Carrisbrook Castle and Queen Victoria's favourite residence, Osborne House, which was most interesting. The Doll's House, specially built for the royal children to play in, was enchanting, the little kitchen and dining-room with the seven chairs around the table, where I imagined all sorts of happy chatter would have taken place.

The amazing rock formations, The Needles, jutting out into the sea. The coloured cliffs skirting the beaches. We were able to collect a little of the coloured sands. We also had a day ticket for the railway which took us practically all over the island. By the time our holiday was over there was very little of the island we had not explored. We certainly had value for money in those days, and I added much to my store of knowledge and education. Margate and Ramsgate was another enjoyable holiday, exploring the surrounding countryside, walking across the Downs to Reculver Towers. We had a whole day in Canterbury, a beautiful old town with the river running through part of it, with the old "Ducking Chair" in view, high up suspended from an old residence over the river bank.

The gem of Canterbury is its beautiful cathedral. I have travelled the length and breadth of England, visited many cathedrals, but my favourite must be Canterbury. There is so much of interest, both inside and out, of structural beauty; it is full of historical events, some very sad, so much more than one could possibly absorb in just one day.

My last planned holiday was to Walmer House, Torquay in 1933, where again I stayed at another of the Christian Alliance Holiday Homes. A beautiful house in a lovely garden, perched high up on the top of a hill. That was a memorable holiday. As soon as my feet were over the threshold I could sense the most wonderful Christian atmosphere that pervaded throughout the house.

I stayed with the family until the summer of 1934, but instead of going on holiday I decided to leave the day that the family went away. I knew I never ever wanted to do any more domestic work for other people, but just how to get away and what to do where accommodation was provided was yet a problem. Giving it a lot of thought and then remembering the happy days working in Shirley Schools' laundry I suddenly thought about more laundry work. I knew there was a large Children's Hospital, in fact the largest in England, at Carshalton, Surrey. I wrote to the matron there asking if she had a vacancy for a laundry worker, which she had. I went for an interview and was accepted on the laundry staff, starting in the summer of 1934.

The accommodation was even better than I had anticipated. Bungalows for living-in staff, separate from the Nurses' Home, with just four people in each, in lovely grounds. All very free and easy. We went to the main dining-rooms for all our meals. I was off duty every evening, from 4 p.m. on Saturday and all day Sunday. What bliss! I felt free at last to organise my own life. I had one special friend I met at the Baptist Church who was also in service and came from Plymouth. Before I left she became engaged to be married and returned to Plymouth. They married in 1936 and have just celebrated their Golden Wedding. They are still my oldest friends. My friends' in-laws had several of their family living at Carshalton Beeches, within walking distance of the Children's Hospital, so they got in touch with them and I was introduced into a wonderful Christian family. Mother, father, three daughters (all unmarried) went to London each day to work. Their married daughter with husband and three small boys lived next door. Another daughter was a missionary in South India. Their houses were almost new with large gardens at the rear, bordering on fields with lots of trees and grazing cattle. In the spring, cowslips, bluebells, buttercups and wild garlic graced the scene, all vying with each other. After summer there were glorious autumn colourings of the trees and always mushrooms in the fields.

I was very happy working with the people in that large laundry. Very much larger than Shirley with more up-to-date machinery. We had lots of fun and all got on well together. It was really hard work, but being happy and contented compensated for the work. With my friends quite near and somewhere to go after work if I wanted to meant a lot to me. I sometimes helped in their garden or with other jobs that needed doing. I was made very welcome with all the family and at their chapel on Sundays.

1934 came to an end, and 1935, into 1936. As I was getting older, my ambitious streak in my make up set me thinking how I could eventually get myself into the nursing profession. I felt I would be doing something worthwhile with my life. How to manage it with just my elementary school education was yet a problem. From the grounds of the Children's Hospital I could see the tower of Banstead Psychiatric Hospital and thought perhaps they would not be quite so fussy about education if the person was keen. I was not thinking of going to Banstead as I knew there were several hospitals in the Epsom area, all psychiatric hospitals, administered by the London County Council. I wrote to two of the matrons in the Epsom area, but never did have a reply. Not wanting to be beaten I finally wrote to the matron of Banstead Hospital, gave two different names and addresses for references, and had a reply within a fortnight, to go for an interview and was accepted to start my training on 6th June 1936. After the interview the assistant matron saw me out with her keys at the side entrance, saying on parting, "How do you think you will get on with your exams?" To be quite honest I had never given exams a thought but without letting on replied, "If other people can pass theirs, I daresay I can." Her reply was, "That's the right spirit", and I made sure that I did! So now I had succeeded in getting on the first rung of the ladder to what turned out to be the happiest period of my early life — happy and contented that I would now be able to make a career for myself, getting a lot of satisfaction, fighting off the disadvantages of my early years. So the great day dawned and I arrived at the hospital after lunch on 6th June 1936, but that's another part of my story.

PART THREE   1936—1944

And the Lord, He it is that doth go before thee.
Deuteronomy 31. v.8

Therefore, go gladly to the task assigned thee.
Having my Promise, needing no-thing more.
Than just to know, where-ere the future find thee.
In all thy journeyings, I go before.

Banstead Hospital was tucked away in a secluded part of Banstead Downs, about two miles from Banstead village, with Belmont village at the bottom of the hill — a truly lovely location. Grassland, trees with wild flowers in profusion growing outside the hospital gates. The hospital had their own farm with cows, pigs, and a large arable section where they grew all their vegetables. I was all set to really enjoy my training there. Several of the new school of trainees had arrived earlier, and the others came before the end of June, in time for the doctors' lectures.

We had a lovely Nurses' Home and all had separate bedrooms. There was always plenty of competition as to who could keep their rooms looking the best, polishing furniture, floors, etc. Two Welsh girls (sisters) each had several pairs of high-heeled shoes polished to perfection, displayed on the tops of their wardrobes, but they spoilt the look of their rooms by covering their polished floors with newspapers.

All our group were on the same floor. At the end of the corridor, hidden away in an alcove, was a gas ring and meter where we could boil a kettle for making tea. We only needed to put one penny in which was plenty for boiling the kettle, but there was always a nurse peeping round the corner waiting for one of us to put the first penny in, then they would be in line to use up the gas that was left.

We were all very apprehensive about going on our wards for the first time. None of our group worked together. My ward was C.2, an Epileptic Ward of sixty patients. My sister-in-charge was an Irish lady. When I arrived she was sitting on a polished wooded bench. While I stood before her, she reeled off a long list of what were to be my duties, saying at the end, "I expect you to remember them". It would have been more than my life was worth to forget anything. However I did appreciate the fact that she was a good disciplinarian. I had got used to discipline all my young life so it did not come hard for me. Our ward was one huge area on the second floor, sixty beds in four rows in the dormitory section, all low beds so that the patients would not hurt themselves should they fall out.

The making of the beds was an art in itself. All were finished off with White counterpanes and made to look like boxes at the ends, absolutely identical with not an inch or a crease out of place. That truly was a sight worth viewing after they were made each morning.

The dining-room went off to the left of the dormitory, with the kitchen behind. Bathroom and toilets at the end of the ward, with the sitting-room in the middle. It was so well planned that it was easy to keep an eye on all the people. The entire place was scrupulously clean. Never before or since have I encountered anything quite like it. You could literally have eaten your food off the floor!

The sitting-room floor was polished with 'Ronuk'. We had great big hand polishers which we swung to and fro, known as 'Dumpers' to finish them off with a good shine. My! weren't they heavy. In my day the nurses in training were responsible for all the cleaning. There were never more than three nurses on duty and quite often only two. When I had been in training for about six weeks, matron decided to do a ward inspection one day when the ward sister was at lunch. She arrived unannounced and I was on duty by myself. As I did the round with matron she asked me the names of all sixty patients. Fortunately I knew them all. I think she may have been assessing my ability as to whether I would make the grade. Well I did, and enjoyed every bit of my training. We had lectures from our Sister Tutor weekly, and learnt a lot about our patients through our work on the wards.

We didn't do any night duty for at least a year after we had taken our Preliminary examination and then for only three months. Although we rarely got moved into other wards we had sufficient experience about all aspects of different types of psychiatric patients and nursing requirements, relieving in other departments including those with specially adapted rooms for the very disturbed ones. The rooms were constructed so that in no way could the patients hurt themselves. The staff always had to get permission from the doctor before they could restrain them. Everything had to be written down and signed by the doctor and ward sister. The patient had to be visited every ten minutes. Two hours was the limit they could be kept in these rooms, after which if still necessary, fresh permission had to be obtained. Never did I see or hear of any patient being ill treated. The smallest scratch or bruise had to be accounted for and investigated. There were no drugs as such during my training, only a mixture known as Paraldehyde which was a sort of sedative and only given when necessary. It was a liquid which most would drink quite happily but it smelt so horrible I could not imagine what it tasted like. The whole hospital absolutely reeked of it. Maybe after the war something more pleasant would have been found for them. I am sure that was the case.

I did my three months' night duty on my own ward. It was summertime and still light when we went on duty each evening. After taking the day report and knowing more or less what could happen during the night, there was not a lot to do after the patients were settled down. Only one nurse was on duty for sixty people. It was made easier for me as I already knew them from day duty. The hospital had a system whereby we had to 'clock in' every hour. One clock was at the top of the ward, the other at the bottom. Both had to be done, which registered on a machine in the night sister's office. We also had two visits from the sister. No nurse dare go to sleep on duty. I usually took something to do when all was quiet, such as letter writing or sewing. After one pay day I bought myself a nice piece of dress material and a pattern, which I cut out in my bedroom ready for tacking together. The very night I took it on duty, matron decided to do the first ward visit. My dress was on the table. Matron picked it up and wanted to know what I was doing. Making a summer dress said I, which she didn't seem to have any objection to. Some weeks later I was getting off the bus at the hospital stop as matron was getting on. It was a nice warm day so I had my new dress on. It was my first attempt at dressmaking and I was feeling very pleased with myself. I was glad when my one and only spell of night duty came to an end. We got very little sleep. One day each week we had to get up for a doctor's lecture at 1.30 p.m. Needless to say sometimes a nurse would 'nod off' during the lecture. Not me though — I never wanted to miss anything.

We took our Preliminary examination after our first year's training, and our Final for 'The Royal Medico Psychological Association Certificate', at the end of our three-year course.

Before the exam results were published, we were given our summer holidays so we left an address where we could be contacted. I went to my friends in Plymouth who invited another friend to come with me. We had a lovely time on Plymouth Hoe, and swimming in the outdoor pool. Another day we went on a boat trip to Looe in Cornwall. When we returned from Looe we found a telegram inside on the door mat congratulating both on passing our Final exam, so we returned jubilant to receive our Certificates. This was July 1939. The General Nursing Council were introducing a State Examination for Psychiatric Nurses. I wanted to go on to take my State General Nurses' training, so decided to have a go at the State Mental Examination. Only two of the staff took it, a male nurse and myself. We both passed first time. I heard later that only five per cent ever managed to pass at the first attempt, so that was an honour for the hospital.

Now 'The World War' was on the verge of starting so I decided to wait until February 1940 to do my SRN. In the meantime I was transferred to our Admission Block, where all new patients were assessed to be transferred after a period of time into their appropriate wards. There we had male and female staff working together.

One afternoon a nurse came to say there was a gentleman looking for me. I could not think who it could be. Turning round there was my brother James whom I had not seen since 1922, looking very smart in soldier's uniform. I was delighted to see him but never had a chance to know how he found out where I was. By this time he was married with a five-year-old son and a baby daughter just a few weeks old. On my next day off I went to London to meet the family. They lived in the Old Kent Road. The war started on 3rd September. Weather-wise it was a glorious late summer. All was quiet for many weeks before the war really erupted.

A lot of our nurse friends became unsettled wondering what they should do: go nearer their homes; get married; or stay put! In fact I think the majority did the latter. The running of the hospital had to go on, war or no war. I was not going to let it interfere with the continuation of my nursing training. I went ahead and applied to Croydon General Hospital to do my training, and went for an interview. The matron only seemed interested as to who my father was, and where I had been educated, so I left with no satisfaction as to whether they would accept me. I then applied to a much smaller Voluntary Hospital, the West Norfolk and Kings Lynn. They didn't ask me to go for an interview, just accepted me on my merits, and deducted six months from my nursing course as I was already a qualified psychiatric nurse. Shortly before I was due to start at Kings Lynn, I received a letter from the matron at Croydon asking me if I was still contemplating doing my training there. I was happy to be able to tell her that I had already been accepted at Kings Lynn.

I started on 1st February 1940. My brother came from London that day to go with me to Liverpool Street Station to see me on the train for Kings Lynn. I was overjoyed at being reunited with him, but my joy was short-lived for that was the last time I saw him.

Kings Lynn is an old river port on the banks of the River Ouse, dividing South Lynn from West Lynn, with many ancient buildings and remnants of town walls — the 15th century South Gate, Tudor Guildhall, 17th century Custom

House on The Wharf; Red Mount Chapel and Greyfriars Tower of a 13th century monastery. The large park bounded by part of the old town wall is known as 'The Walks', through which we could walk to South Gate and across the river bridge to West Lynn. The majority of the population of West Lynn were arable farmers. Sugar-beet was a great industry providing work for a great number of people in the processing factory in Kings Lynn. Strawberries were grown by the acre in fields outside the town. The local people looked forward to the picking season to make some extra income for themselves.

We had a very good training at our hospital although it was tough at times with the war on, having to cope with civilian and service casualties. There were several small airfields dotted around Norfolk, Cambridge and Lincolnshire. When possible on our days off we escaped into the countryside around Sandringham. Masses of rhododendrons, ferns and heathers on the heathland made a colourful display in early summer and autumn. Surrounding Sandringham House were several beautiful avenues of mature trees of many varieties, copper beech, elm, oak, chestnut and pine, providing a wonderful playground for the squirrels. West Newton village where many of the estate workers lived, was a haven of peace with their lovely stone cottages and beautifully-kept gardens.

We had several hospital exams to take during our training before we took our final SRN at the Norfolk and Norwich Hospital in Norwich. The night before there had been a terrible air raid, so we thought the exam would be postponed, but that was not so. We went the forty miles by train, arriving to find all round the hospital bombed buildings, fire hoses, and water everywhere. We had to pick our way through all that to get inside the hospital. Waiting for the exam results seemed endless. I reckoned under such disturbing circumstances we all deserved to pass, which we did.

I made a lot of friends at Banstead and Kings Lynn and was sorry to leave them. Only two of us did not marry, a friend who lived in Blackburn and myself. Several friends still keep in touch after fifty years.

Despite the war I wanted to do my midwifery training in London so I applied to do Part One at a hospital in

Greenwich, but could only do it on condition that I did six months nursing at the hospital first. The top floor of the hospital had been evacuated because of the air raids, so I worked in a thirty-bedded medical ward on the ground floor which was a very busy unit. That period finished, I was then able to start my midwifery training.

Greenwich was just a tram ride from where my brother's family lived, so one afternoon I went to see them. That was the only time I found them in. On the way back to Greenwich it was getting dark so a kind policeman shepherded me across the road and advised me to go back on the Underground instead of the tram. When I got to the Underground Station I was not prepared for what confronted me. It was crowded with people all carrying blankets and possessions preparing to spend the night in the Underground. Some had already claimed their places with beds already made up, as there were raids nearly every night. Underground platforms are cold draughty places at the best of times. The memories of all those poor people, young and old, packed into that Underground remained with me for a very long time.

I went back twice in 1943 to the Old Kent Road to visit the family, but never found anyone there. I then enquired of a neighbour if my sister-in-law was still living there. The neighbour, not knowing who I was, said she didn't live here now. Her husband was killed, and she has gone with her two children to live with her mother in Sunderland. So that was how I heard the sad news. I was never notified of my brother's death, not being considered next of kin. Over the years I have been through innumerable channels trying to find the family, but so far without success.

By now I had almost completed my Part One training, and after the exam results came through I left London to do Part Two at Epsom, Surrey. It was a nice new Maternity Unit on the edge of Epsom Downs. Three months was spent in the hospital and the last three on the district at Cheam with the Queens District Nursing Association. One evening when I was on night duty and just about 10 p.m. when we were taking the babies from the nursery to their mothers for their last feed, the air-raid siren sounded. Then there was an almighty bang! A bomb had dropped quite near and all the

Our sports group, Shirley Schools, Croydon, Surrey 1921. With Mr Roberts, Headmaster; Miss Capes, Matron; Mr Small, Sports Master. Competing against Addiscombe Girls School, Shirley winning the Shield. Myself in the centre holding it.

Myself sitting in an ornamental alcove of our Nurses' Home, 1937.

In a friend's garden at Carshalton beeches with "Bimbo", one of the hospital kittens who needed a good home.

Prize Giving Day at the West Norfolk & Kings Lynn Hospital, 1942. Doctors, Matron and nursing staff, with a representative from the Royal College of Nursing.

Prize Giving Day at the West Norfolf & Kings Lynn Hospital, 1942. Doctors, Matron and nursing staff, with a representative from the Royal College of Nursing.

*At Flete Maternity Unit, Lord Mildmay's Estate 1944—1946,
for the benefit of the Press.
We were only pretending to be picking the daffodils!*

Albion Street House, Kingston-upon-Hull, East Yorkshire (now known as North Humberside). Part Two Training School for Midwives, 1948.

*My brother, James Down. Taken just before the 1939—1945 war.
He was a Corporal in the Middlesex Regiment
and died on active service, April 1943.
His name is on the Memorial Roll of Honour.*

lights went out. I already had one baby in my arms but there were another two in the nursery, so I did what we were told never to do: 'Carry more than one baby at a time'. I quickly gathered the other two in my arms and groped my way along the dark passage just in case anything should happen to them, and gave them to their right mothers. We left the babies with their mothers until the 'All Clear' sounded much later that night.

My three months' training soon passed, and then I went to my district at Cheam, which I loved. It was so nice delivering babies in their own homes, and looking after them for another two weeks. The Queens nurses had motor bikes to get around the district. Pupils had ordinary bicycles which we had to buy ourselves. I had never had a bicycle so I found them difficult to ride. In fact I never did master them. I could never take my hand off the handlebars to ring the bell! I was more often walking with my bike than riding it.

By this time the dreaded Doodle-Bugs or Flying Bombs as some people called them were descending upon us. I believe the very first one dropped at Ewell, a village on the outskirts of Epsom town. One evening I was returning from a case when I heard a Doodle-Bug coming over. They had a distinctive sound and you knew as soon as the engine cut out that it would be only a matter of seconds before it dropped. I dived behind a garden hedge until it was safe to come out. Another day, about 6 p.m., after finishing work for the day, as I thought, I decided to have a bath before the evening meal. My bedroom was near the bathroom but no sooner had I got into the bath than I heard a Doodle-Bug approaching. I had to move quickly and just got my dressing-gown on in time. Should I go into my bedroom or sit on the top of the stairs which were nearer? I just made the stairs! The bomb dropped at the junction of three roads in North Cheam. The elegant bay windows in the lounge of our house, which were very large almost from the ceiling to garden level, fell in like a pack of cards! When I eventually went into my bedroom, half the ceiling had come down onto the bed. What a mess. Thank goodness no one in the house was hurt. Outside, the roads were littered with broken glass, bricks and slates off roofs. There were at least four hundred houses damaged.

C

Another afternoon during an air raid I had to go to a case at North Cheam. By the time I arrived the lady had gone down to her air-raid shelter at the bottom of her garden in which she had a single bed, so I had no alternative but to deliver her baby there. This lady I remember had an eighteen-year-old daughter, and was fostering a little Greek boy who she was very fond of. I think she was hoping for a son of her own, but she had another daughter. However, all went well, and soon mother and baby were back in their home.

So now my District Training came to an end and I returned to Epsom to take my Final exam. By September 1944 I had completed all the training I had set out to achieve when I first started nursing in June 1936. I was successful in all my exams, acquiring five Certificates. I was very grateful to the matron at Banstead for giving me my first opportunity of making a career for myself.

Eight years of training had all been worthwhile, very satisfying and rewarding. I could truly say,

'I can do all things through Christ which strengtheneth me.'

Philippians 4. v.13.

PART FOUR   1944—1952

>My God I thank Thee
>Who has made the earth, so bright.
>So full of splendour, joy and Truth.
>Beauty and light.
>So many glorious things are here,
>Noble and right.

September 1944 was decision time. The war not yet over, but I being a free agent, could make plans for my next venture. I wanted to get more experience nursing in the different counties, and getting to know more about my England. To start with if possible, getting a midwife's post in Plymouth. During the war all qualified nurses had to continue with whatever branch of nursing they were doing until the war ended. I applied to Plymouth and was appointed as a staff midwife at Freedom Fields Hospital. When I arrived Plymouth city centre was in ruins. St. Andrew's Church, the principal church, was just a shell, as was Charles Street Church, only a short distance away. The tower alone now stands as a memorial to a great number of Plymothians who lost their lives when an underground shelter one night in Charles Street had a direct hit from a large bomb. Long after the war, St. Andrew's was rebuilt. In the meantime services were held within its walls, open to the sky. It is now one of the finest churches in the west country and well worth visiting.

Much of Plymouth city centre remained in ruins for years. Eventually rebuilding got underway. The very narrow streets with their shops and open markets became wide roads with modern buildings, losing all their wonderful character of bygone days. Sentiment had to give way to progress. There are still a few of the old buildings left, for instance, the Guildhall and Treasury. It was a miracle that Plymouth Hoe remained intact, also 'Drakes' Island' out in The Sound. From The Hoe one has wonderful views from the gardens, war memorial, and Smeatons Tower, an old lighthouse dismantled from a rocky outcrop on the coast, which was rebuilt on The Hoe. On a fine day the breakwater can be seen a couple of miles out, keeping the rough waters of the channel from encroaching into The Sound. A great many houses surrounding The Hoe were demolished in the blitz. Elliott Terrace, where Lady Astor had a fine residence, escaped damage. My friends lived on the edge of town, so all they got was one incendiary bomb through their roof, which was quickly dealt with. They turned their cellar into an air-raid shelter which had a solid concrete floor, and electric lighting which could not be seen from outside, and plenty of room for assembling deck-chairs to sit in. They spent many a night there.

I only worked at Freedom Fields Hospital for two weeks, then was sent out to their Maternity Annex at Flete House, situated in beautiful grounds twelve miles from Plymouth. How delighted I was to get into such beautiful countryside. Flete House served the whole of South Devon including Plymouth and was a Part One Training School, the pupils coming to us after doing their first three months at the hospital.

We were surrounded by farmland, and the lovely villages of Holbeton, Ford, Modbury, Ugborough and Ermington. From Ermington village with its fine old church with a crooked spire, the River Erme wends its way through meadows and under a bridge on the main Kingsbridge Road into the Flete Estate, where it yet had another two miles to flow before joining the sea at Mothecombe Bay.

The beauty of that estate was beyond description. Along the river banks in springtime were masses of double flowering snowdrops, primroses and violets. On the other side a pedestrian walk beside the river in wooded countryside carpeted with bluebells and celandines leading right down to the sea. The gardens surrounding the entrance to the house were a picture, with daffodils, camellias, rhododendrons, and countless clusters of trees on grassy slopes.

Inside was a magnificent entrance hall and staircase. We only used part of the house which was separated from the private family apartments. I had been at Flete about eight months when the war ended in May 1945. We were all very excited that an announcement was to be given at 3.30 p.m. on that day. There was no television then, but we had a radio in our dining-room, so we rushed downstairs, standing around waiting to hear the good news. When it came we all cheered in tune with the crowds in London which came over loud and clear. Our sister-in-charge was curled up in an armchair with a book — an avid reader. Without moving she just said, 'Nothing but mass hysteria!'

I stayed at Flete for another year after the war ended. We took turns doing night duty but only for short periods at a time. Once the war was over we relaxed, and with that beautiful estate to wander around in our off duty, it was heaven. I simply loved everything about the place, including my work.

Going on duty at 8.30 one evening I had a feeling it was going to be a busy night with all the new admissions during the day. What an exciting night it turned out to be. I was the only qualified person on duty, with two pupils, and twenty or more mothers and babies to look after. At 9.30 p.m. on 1st May, the first baby was born. Six more arrived after midnight on 2nd May between 1 a.m., and the last at 6.30 a.m. So there were seven new arrivals by morning, all bathed and tucked up snug in their cots by the time the day staff came on duty. Four boys. Three girls. Six from Plymouth, and one from a nearby village. I claimed this to have been the happiest night's work of my life. There was always a lot of writing to be done for each case, so it was almost lunch-time before I got off duty. I left Flete in July 1946 to be with my Plymouth friend who was expecting her second baby, who arrived on 8th August.

My next move was back to a lovely rural area in Norfolk, as a district nurse midwife. I did general nursing, midwifery, health visiting and was responsible for all the elderly people in the Alms Houses. I had accommodation in one of the estate cottages, with a middle-aged married couple. The only snag was that the area I was expected to cover with a bicycle, was far too large. The district nurses in the rural areas were controlled by local committees. There was a car for the nurse but not much help to me who had never driven one. However, I got a Provisional licence, determined to master it, with a bit of verbal tuition from the garage where I got petrol and had repairs done. The car was an old green Austin Seven which was always going wrong, with a luggage rack tied on the back. One summer's evening when I knew the roads would be quiet, I took the car out on my own, crossed the main Norwich Road and went off into the country. A few miles on, turning round a large tree in a village square, I took a wrong turning and found myself in a narrow road with cattle in fields on either side. Fortunately there was a farm worker in the field who gave me instructions on how to get back, but when I told him I could not turn the car round in the narrow road, he was highly amused, jumped in and turned it for me. I got back without any mishaps. After that I had gained a lot of confidence and drove with a Provisional licence all the time I was there, even going into town occasionally. Not much fun at night though, going across commons to midwifery cases. Having to get out of the car opening and shutting gates. Driving along unlit roads with dykes on either side. It was lovely in spring and summer, but not that awful winter of 1947, when the snow was six feet high along both sides of the slippery roads for weeks on end. One lady was expecting twins in the January when the snow was at its worst, so I asked her husband if he would come for me if I was wanted. Sure enough on 8th January the phone rang at 2.15 a.m. Their cottage was very small with just one fireplace. There was a lovely fire when I arrived. The only means of heating water was with kettles and saucepans on the open fire. The babies' cot was made up beside the fire with hot-water bottles for extra warmth. David and Brian arrived an hour later, within ten minutes of each other, both weighing 7lbs. 4ozs. Their nine-year-old sister was delighted, also parents and grandma. They were a very happy family, and the babies did well despite the cold weather.

Later that year I was on new ground, going to Kingston-upon-Hull in East Yorkshire, to a Part Two Midwifery Training School. There were twelve pupils, one sister, and matron. We all lived in one large house, and worked all the centre of Hull, the poorest part, but I loved it. Never a dull moment. There were hundreds of little terraced houses, some with just one room upstairs, and one down, with a little scullery at the rear. The people were very poor, mostly with big families. We used to take our own soap and pennies for the phone box should we need to use one. Hull was the only place with its own telephone system, and despite Telecom, I believe still is.

Hull was a very interesting place, very flat and near several seaside places. When I was there the population were mostly fisher folk with their great boats that got as far as the Arctic regions. Now there is hardly any fishing done. Just the same there was a variety of industry: a cocoa factory; surgical instruments; Elastoplast; fish curing; several swing bridges over the rivers and other waterways, providing a lot of employment; and outside the town there were many farms.

Although the war had been over for two years, much evidence of the bombing still remained. The tall statue of their famous son, William Wilberforce who in his day did so much for the abolition of slavery, was standing undamaged in the middle of the Town Square, in summer surrounded by flower-beds in full bloom. The winters were very severe, with lots of snow and at odd times we had to dig our bicycles out of a snow-drift when out on a case at night, and had to keep the only water tap in the backyard running for fear it should freeze up. I always liked a Christmas baby, so I went out to the case myself instead of sending anyone else. When I got the call one Christmas morning, I found that the mother had no clothes at all for the new arrival. Two neighbours came to my rescue and went round a few houses collecting what they could, so by the time the baby was born at 11.30 a.m. there were plenty of clothes for the lovely baby girl. She could not have been better dressed. It really is amazing how neighbours will help out in an emergency. I worked in Hull for over two years, then went to Stoke-on-Trent in the Potteries — Arnold

Bennett's 'Five Towns' — doing district midwifery. It was before the Clean Air Regulations came into force. The air was so full of soot from the numerous kilns, heated by coal which fired the china. No one could hang washing out to dry, it would be covered with soot in seconds. There was also coal-mining in the area. The people were all very friendly. I lived at a place called Shelton between Hanley and Burslem. Although this was a very dirty part of Staffordshire the area outside the town was very nice, and in no time you could get to Trentham Gardens, or on the other side of town to Congleton, and the beautiful Derbyshire Dales. The grime alone drove me back to the South and to Beckenham, Kent Maternity Hospital, where I was in charge of the clinics until March 1952. By the time I left Beckenham another eight years of my life had gone by since my training days, but I had gleaned a lot along the way.

For many years I had a hankering to leave England and work in Australia as I had read several books about the country which fascinated me. Knowing that I could never muster enough money for my travels, I wrote to Australia House to see if I could emigrate. With a career behind me I had no trouble at all being accepted, so all arrangements were completed before I left Beckenham.

My friend in Buckinghamshire was having another baby and had already asked me if I could take on her case before going to Australia. So I left to be with her before the end of March. The family lived in what had once been G. K. Chesterton's house, called 'Top Meadow' in Beaconsfield. Easter was late that year, and very cold, with a snowstorm raging when the baby arrived on Good Friday afternoon, 11th April. So now with everything settled I stayed with my friend until a few days before leaving from Tilbury Docks on the Pacific-Orient line via Suez to Fremantle. I was very much looking forward to what I hoped would turn into a great adventure.

PART FIVE   1952—1955

Tis good to dwell on things
    Which cannot perish.
Which cannot change, nor fade,
    Nor yet decay.
Those things which, deep within,
    We truly cherish.
And which can never, never
    Pass away.

I made my way alone to Tilbury on the day of departure for Australia in April 1952, not one bit afraid of the unknown. The Lord had led me thus far, and I knew He would still lead me on. I was very much looking forward to my journey to a land I had read a lot about, and was now longing to explore.

Our boat, being one for migrants only, was full to capacity. There were ten of us sharing a cabin but we only went to it at bedtime, finding plenty to do on the boat and watching all that went on. I was having a good rest after all my hard work over the years.

It was cold and blustery on deck, but as long as there was a vestige of the English landscape to see, I stayed to watch it recede from sight. When I went into our large dining-room for our first meal, I was delighted to find a lovely bouquet of flowers from some of my colleagues at Beckenham Hospital, so I decorated them into one of the ship's vases and had them on our dining-table for many days before they faded.

The weather improved and warmed up considerably as we made our way out of the Channel and on towards the

Mediterranean. It was a beautifully sunny day as we approached Gibraltar and were near enough to be able to see the Barbary Apes on 'The Rock'. We then made for Port Said where we were held up for some time.

Trouble was brewing in Suez, so while the boat remained anchored we were able to go ashore and have a look around. After about forty-eight hours we finally got away, and were almost the last of the craft who made it before the Suez Canal closed, and remained closed for many years.

It was very hot going through the Canal, but much fresher entering the Indian Ocean, and across to Ceylon, now known as Sri Lanka. We anchored there for several hours in beautiful weather. The sea was as blue as the sky above. From there we continued on to Australia, and berthed at Fremantle early one morning towards the end of May.

Coming into their winter season, it was still quite warm. There was much activity as everyone was getting off the boat. The passengers were mostly families going out to settle. There were buses waiting to convey us to the different camps, where we could stay for a fortnight with free board and accommodation. Ours was a small campsite in a country setting a few miles from Perth with a lot of silver birch trees, where I heard my first kookaburra. The accommodation was all of corrugated iron. Each bed had a mosquito net fitted; the mosquitoes were not the malarial type, but we were glad to have them to keep the flies off. There was a very nice dining area and the food was good. The camp was run by a homely married couple who were most helpful.

I think some of the people would have taken advantage of the two weeks' free board, but within forty-eight hours I was off to Perth to see what I could find to do.

My first stop was to the office of the Chief Nursing Officer to see what she had to offer but she only had a position in a small bush hospital 200 miles from Perth. I thought about it over the weekend, and in the meantime went to the office of a Private Nursing Association, where they only had one case, that of taking a lady from hospital to her daughter's home by ambulance, to a place called Pinjarra, sixty miles from Perth in the wheat belt. I returned to the camp for another day to pack up, then went back to Perth after the weekend. This I thought would be a start which might lead to something else. I had no idea what to expect going sixty miles out of town, but it turned out to be a very nice brick bungalow with all modern amenities in its own grounds. The whole area was overrun by rabbits, hundreds of them.

They were a very nice family and the daughter was a marvellous cook. She made such tasty meals, and I will never forget those sweet potatoes which she roasted. They were quite delicious. Unfortunately for the family their mother only lived just over a fortnight, as she had cancer. The family invited me to stay on for a while so I had another two weeks with them. Then I returned to Perth and stayed at a Nurses' Holiday Home for a few days to have a look round Perth, and also to see if I could find anything to do, but without success. I asked the lady where I was staying if she knew of anyone who might be able to help. She did happen to know of a matron in charge of a home for retired soldiers from the 1914—1918 War, who would telephone the house when she was short of staff, but nobody wanted that sort of work. Then one day while I was still there she did phone, so I said I would go. Better than not working at all.

Western Australia is the largest of all the states, and Perth is truly beautiful. The lovely Swan River, Kings Park of many acres, the town and shopping centre, and the many miles of beautiful beaches with their white sand all around the coastline. The Soldiers' Home was about six miles out by bus from Perth. Not a township, or hamlet, just one large house which I should imagine had been a private family home, set in the country. Across the road was a single line railway. There were no shops, just one little Post Office on the other side of the railway. I never saw a train at all, only lots of goannas always along both sides of the railway track, quite harmless.

There were thirty or more gentlemen at the Home. The Australian Government certainly know how to look after their ex-servicemen. They lived in grand conditions. There was very little nursing needed. Just a matter of keeping an eye on them, and seeing they were well looked after. All I seemed to do was wash socks, mend socks, wash and iron shirts, turn collars of shirts when they frayed, give out packets of sweets and tobacco, daily. Those that were able helped around the

Home, several in the kitchen. Just outside the kitchen was a tall tree, and an old cut-down tree trunk, which the kookaburras knew all about! At a certain time each day they would congregate in the tree and start laughing. Their laughter was so infectious I wanted to laugh with them. That was the signal for the men who worked in the kitchen to come out with some meat which they cut up on the old tree trunk. The birds would then come down and help themselves. This was a daily occurrence. They also had a cat who came in each morning for his breakfast of cake!

One afternoon when I was off duty I went for a walk in the bush, all part of the estate. I wandered alone enjoying the solitude when suddenly I came across an animal cemetery hidden away where no one would ever expect to find such a place. There were, I should think, over thirty little tombstones, all with their pets' names engraved on them, and some with little verses of affection. Mostly dogs, but also some cats. I imagined them to have been a typical English family who had settled there, having loved their pets, but sad at their departure. On my way back, looking at all the things around me, I heard a rustling of something coming through the grass. Turning round there was the largest goanna I had seen. I just stood still. He opened his mouth and spat at me just like our domestic cats do when angry. Somehow animals seem to sense people who like them and would do them no harm. He just turned and ambled away.

I stayed several months at the Home and enjoyed looking after the gentlemen, and the daily visits of the kookaburras, but still kept my eye on the advertisements in the local paper. Then one morning I saw that a midwife was required at the Queen Victoria Hospital, Launceston, Tasmania. Just the sort of work I was looking for, so wrote to the matron right away and was appointed to start in December. My fare to Tasmania was to be refunded when I left the hospital.

After working two weeks' notice I set off for Melbourne towards the end of November, and on 1st December went overnight by boat across the Bass Strait to Burnie, Tasmania. It was a very rough crossing. All the passengers had a sleeping berth but we were glad when the journey was over. From Burnie I travelled by bus about one hundred miles to Launceston.

All the places along the route had English names. Launceston was on the River Tamar and we passed a pretty township by the name of Devonport. I arrived at the Queen Victoria Hospital in late afternoon of 2nd December. It was a fairly large and busy place, but I soon settled down. We had an extremely nice matron who was very kind and considerate to all her staff, quite the nicest matron I had ever worked under. There were several Inter-State nurses on the staff. I was the only one from England. Most of us wanted to see as much of Tasmania as possible. We were allowed to save up our weekly days off so that we could have several together to do our sightseeing. There was a very nice cottage on the coast which I think belonged to the matron, so occasionally some of the staff were able to go there for a weekend. The wildlife along that coast was exciting with many differing types of birds, and colonies of seals on the rocky outcrops.

Tasmania is the most English of the states with a variety of scenery. Launceston is in the north, Hobart in the south, with Mount Wellington overseeing the whole town, coated with snow in the winter. The Huon and Derwent Valleys with their miles of apple orchards were a glorious sight in blossom time. There are many typical English churches and houses all with English names. Port Arthur, the old convict settlement out on the Tasman Peninsula where so many of our people were confined in the early days, was now after so many years just a ruin, kept more as a museum piece.

In the north of the island, up in the hills was Queenstown, only reached by a rack-railway. This was the journey I took, winding the way up very slowly through thick bush country into the copper mining area, all very interesting.

Coming back from one of my jaunts by bus, we drove through a road where there had been a severe bush fire, but which had been extinguished. The trunks of the large trees which had been left to slowly burn themselves out, looked like huge torches in the dwindling twilight. It was a fantastic sight. Another time when I was unable to get back, I stayed overnight at an hotel, arriving about 4.30 p.m. When I went into the visitors' lounge it was full of men listening to the radio. Then I realised they were listening to England playing the last day of the Test Match (1953) hoping to regain The Ashes. Being a cricket fan I was very interested, and stayed to listen. One by one the men disappeared when they knew which side was winning, so I was left alone to hear the final verdict. Great News! England had regained The Ashes.

Soon after arriving in Tasmania I met a lady at the church I went to. She was housekeeper to an English family close by, so we would often see each other. One time when I had a weekend off we arranged to go to King Island which was fifty miles out in the Bass Strait. There was a ferry boat which went across twice a week, also a small aircraft which took two passengers, so we went by air to Currie, the only township with the only airstrip. The island is forty miles long and sixteen miles across. We did not know that anything special was taking place on the island, and thought it would be easy enough to get accommodation, but when we arrived we discovered it to be their yearly Mutton-bird weekend gathering. The Mutton-bird is like a small duck which hollows out its nest in hedges, laying just one egg. Our enquiries brought no help at all. All accommodation was fully booked, so I suggested we look for the policeman's house to see if he could help. We found that he had a nice bungalow, with his wife and two children. Very reluctantly he said we could stay there, but never even offered us a cup of tea. We had to go out to a small cafe for our breakfast the next morning, and all other meals during our stay. The aircraft was not due back for two days, so we just had a good walk over part of the island. The weather was very cold and windy.

King Island is better known for all the tragic shipwrecks that have happened around its coast. My little book about King Island (*Echoes of the Past*, 2nd edn.) tells me of at least fifty-seven wrecks between 1801 and 1934, although the majority occurred before the two lighthouses were installed — Wickham Light Tower, high up on the northern extremity, and Currie Lighthouse, midway along the west coast.

I enjoyed my work at the hospital very much. All mothers had their babies in hospital, booked by local doctors, who liked to be there when the babies were born. It was a work of art getting them there in time, but somehow I managed to.

We had a very nice park near the hospital, with all English trees, and a few tame wallabies roaming about. They would eat out of our hands. I stayed in Tasmania almost a year seeing all the seasons through. When I left, as well as my wages, I was given a double fare to Melbourne, so I felt quite rich. I returned by air, as I could not face another rough boat trip across the Bass Strait.

After a short stay in Melbourne, I returned to Sydney, which centres around its great deep water harbour, with its two and a half million people. While twenty-two magnificent ocean beaches offer a cool escape to city dwellers each weekend, I visited Bondi Beach, famous for its life-saving and surfing. Also Manly, another very popular place. Sydney Harbour Bridge is a fantastic sight. It has a single span of over 1,600 feet, eight traffic lanes, two rail tracks, cycle and footpaths. Even an Observation Pylon for great views, and now the wonderful looking Opera House on the water's edge. It was while I was in Sydney that I found another nursing post advertised for Kiama, seventy-four miles from Sydney on the south coast of New South Wales. It was in the gentle green hills with farming land and grazing cattle within sight of the sea. Kiama was a small township, with no public transport other than the railway, and a district hospital, with a separate maternity unit. I worked on the General Nursing side. All the staff, other than myself, were Australians. We worked well together.

The surrounding countryside was beautiful. Jamberoo, Aborigine for 'a track', a small hamlet, was my special favourite, a good mile away, but a lovely walk. Since my day many new homes have been built in that area to enable young married people to live on their own home ground. Wollongong, ten miles down the coast, is a big industrial town where many people from miles around are employed. While I was at Kiama, it was the nearest I would ever be to Canberra, the Australian Capital Territory, only about 200 miles away, so I was not going to miss the chance of seeing it. Canberra is a city planned and created solely as a centre of government, with its wide streets and fine civic buildings, set in flat scrub land, home of many Embassies as well as the Australian Parliament. It was only in its infancy at that time, not completely finished, and the 6,000 trees that had been planted were still quite small. I just had to imagine how lovely they would look a few years hence. When I left Kiama in April 1954, I was now off to see the Northern Territory, and the great outback of Australia, not really knowing where it would eventually lead me. But what an exciting adenture it turned into.

Returning to Sydney I booked a four-day coach tour to Brisbane, in Queensland, along what is known as the Pacific Highway, passing through all the principal towns of northern New South Wales, full of interest and variety. Leaving the bustle of Sydney Town behind, we motored along the banks of the lovely Hawkesbury River, on through mile upon mile of citrus orchards. Then the scene changed to pineapple groves planted on slopes, to get the full benefit of the morning sun. Banana plantations, acres of sugar cane, all the way through to Queensland. It was lovely to see such a variety of produce growing.

I travelled through all these places several weeks after a cyclone had raged around the coast with its resulting devastation and floods, which occurred about a week after the Queen's visit to the area. There was still much evidence of the flooding everywhere. Many small bridges had been washed away. Alternative routes had to be found. Debris was piled high along the fences, and in one place a house was lying completely on its side. At Lismore, a small hamlet, a child's cot was lodged securely in the topmost branches of a tall tree, which was still standing. Grafton, one of the largest of the townships, is divided by a bridge spanning the River Clarence, a very popular place during its jacaranda season. They have the loveliest jacaranda avenue running the whole length of the main street, which when I was there, was a wonderful sight, masses of blue blossom, with inevitably a carpet of blue petals beneath. People come from all parts of Australia to their Jacaranda Festival, which takes place about October. From Grafton our journey took us through Tweed Heads, and crossed the boundary of New South Wales in Queensland, at Coolangatta, a famous surfing and holiday resort, with a glorious expanse of coastline.

A few miles further on we stopped at Surfers' Paradise where I went into the zoo to see 'Topsy', the talking pony. Then another two hours journey brought us into Brisbane.

The Brisbane River, spanned by three attractive bridges, lends a fine setting to the town built around it. There are some very fine buildings, the Botanical Gardens, and lake, home for lots of black swans with their bright red beaks. I spent four days in Brisbane exploring it pretty thoroughly. One day I went to 'Lone-Pine', the Koala Bear Sanctuary, which was very enjoyable. The koalas are such adorable cuddly little bears, but completely expressionless.

My next important thing was a visit to their tourist office. I told the gentleman in charge that I would like to see as much of Australia as possible. Could he work out an itinerary for me? He was most helpful, but first wanted to know what had made me want to go to Australia in the first place. That was easily answered. I told him that I had read several of Neville Shute's books: *A Town Like Alice* and others, including *In the Wet*. He said I could not have had a better reason. Then he produced a large map of Australia, and showed me part of the wild Australian outback of which *In the Wet* was written about, adding that was where he was born. With the map before me I was able to see exactly where I wanted to go, and when I got to Darwin (on the map) I happened to say wouldn't it be wonderful if I could go all around that northwest coast, back to Fremantle. He told me it could be done, but there was only one boat that went, which could only take twelve passengers, and was always fully booked. However he suggested that when I got to Darwin I went to their tourist office and enquire as to whether there had been any passenger cancellations, which I wasted no time in doing the very first morning after my arrival. To my delight there had been just the one, which I was able to have. So I had an enjoyable two weeks going all round that coast in perfect weather conditions, sunshine all the way.

I had a wonderful itinerary mapped out for me. All accommodation and transport was arranged. The boat journey from Darwin to Fremantle was organised the same day as my enquiry. From Brisbane, I started by travelling a 100 miles inland to Toowoomba, crossing 'The Great Dividing Range'. I had four weeks to spare there, so found some work, and did a holiday relieving post at Oakey Hospital, only a very small place, another nineteen miles further on in the wheat belt, on Darling Downs. I was sorry it was such a short stay, but my time was all mapped out, so I had to be on my way again, back to Brisbane, to take the night train to Mackay, another 600 miles, up the coast from where I did a five-day cruise of the Great Barrier Reef. The boat, *Roylan I*, was skippered by the captain who owned it, and with his crew were one happy family. We visited all the islands out in the Whitsunday Passage, Brampton, Haymen, Daydream, Lindeman, South Molle and Mandalay. On Brampton there was a herd of goats, and it was fascinating to see them standing for long periods in the shallow water, early in the morning.

Mandalay looked so very picturesque from the boat. Just one dwelling, painted white, with a bright red roof, and tropical fruits and flowers growing right down to the water's edge. We went across to the island in small motor boats. As we were approaching four little dogs came dashing down to greet us, thinking our main object was to play with them. There was one room in the house kept solely for the most beautifully arranged collection of coral (not for sale) of every colour and shape, some representing colourful flowers.

Our boat anchored each night and always for meals, so it was very restful. One day we went out to the Coral Reef, but as the tide was in viewed the coral through glass-bottomed boats. It was a wonderful sight to see hundreds of small multi-coloured fish swimming in and out of the coral beds, combining to make a perfect picture. Between times we fished from the boat. All tackle was supplied, just hooks and lines. For the first two days I caught nothing and was about to give up in despair, when I caught a fair-sized grey nurse shark. That same evening I hooked a much larger fish. I had to call for assistance to help heave it in. Two passengers came to my rescue, but when we got it to within a foot of the deck, it made one almighty struggle for freedom and slipped back into the water. The next day I caught a crimson government bream, and a rainbow trout, so didn't think that was too bad for my first fishing venture, but that was to be the last, for I cannot bear the thought of destroying such beautiful things of nature.

I was sorry when that glorious cruise came to an end, but

the enjoyable memories will linger long, of happy days spent among some of God's most perfect handiwork of nature and colour. The very first chapter of the Bible reminds us in verses 25 and 31, 'God saw everything that he had made, and behold, *it was very good*'. Returning to Mackay, I boarded the night train for Cairns, arriving twenty-four hours later. The journey was very enjoyable, and the land was much more fertile and green than I had imagined it would be, passing through many little townships with their mandarin and orange groves.

Cairns itself was not nearly as large a place as I had thought, so I soon got around to seeing all the things of interest in the area. The most interesting afternoon was spent at a private house, viewing a shell collection, 10,000 of them from all over the world. It had taken the lady owner five years to arrange them. Her husband had risen to the occasion and made her some very nice cabinets with shallow drawers which showed them off to perfection. Sixteen miles up in the hills from Cairns is Kuranda, a small isolated township. The journey was by an electric railway climbing up through the Ranges, suddenly emerging from stone tunnels to look out over fertile valleys of swaying sugar cane and patchwork fields of other crops. On one side, the Stony Creek Falls dash down from a height of over 1,000 feet, while just three miles from Kuranda, the Barron Falls, where the train always stops to allow visitors to get out to see the magnificent views, and take photographs.

Kuranda is the terminus of the railway and the station is a real gem. The station-master took a great interest in it and had the most wonderful collection of plants and ferns growing in the gardens, and hanging from the platforms, all the way round the station; while a white rustic bridge added extra charm to its setting. I only had three weeks to spare before continuing my journey, so I found work at the hotel. It was very hard work as I had to do a bit of everything, including washing bed linen — no washing-machines or spin-dryers. The drying lines were tied from trees in a meadow, with the grass knee-high, and a few banana trees scattered about. The weather was lovely so hanging out sheets, etc. dripping wet, soon dried. One afternoon I wandered out to a place called Paradise. Leaving the main road I skirted the garden of a private house, took a track across two fields, and found myself following a creek which I continued along for about a quarter of a mile, and suddenly found myself in the heart of a forest, surrounded by umbrella ferns, which really do look like big tall umbrellas. In the centre of this was a hut with brightly-painted seats and tables, where one could sit in the quietness, while enjoying freshly-made tea and home-made cakes. The elderly lady offered to row me back across the river after serving tea, as she said it was easier than the way I had come.

When I set off with her I discovered we had about a mile to walk before we reached the Barron River. It was a most instructive and interesting nature study lesson I was in for, the lady knowing everything about the forest and all the different types of trees and plants along the way. The sun was just about setting as I stepped off the boat at Kuranda. I managed to get on camera a nice impression in colour of evening on the Barron River, with my nature study teacher rowing the boat back to its mooring. Before leaving Kuranda I visited the Atherton Tablelands, thus seeing another aspect of Queensland. After another short stay in Cairns, I journeyed south by train to Townsville from where I took 'The Sunlander', an air-conditioned train, 603 miles to Mount Isa, and the terminus of the Queensland Railway. The journey was entirely different to any I had yet encountered, which gave me an insight into the vast uninhabited wilderness of the outback. Early the following morning, as I looked out through the train window, with the hot sun rising in the heavens shedding its glimmering rays over the dried-up barren wilderness, the whole scene presented one of utter desolation. Yet at the same time one could not help feeling a great admiration for the few who toil and live under conditions that most people would shun. The only dwellings visible during that 603 mile journey were those of the railway workers who kept the track in good repair. Mount Isa was reached at 6 p.m., so I made straight for the hotel, a meal, and an early night.

I had to spend two days there. Not a very nice place. Abounding in dust, dirt and flies. Its only industry was silver, lead and copper mining, where almost without exception, the entire population worked, and spend their leisure and money, in the public house. We were awakened early on the morning of our departure and had tea and toast before our bus left at 6 a.m. Our final destination for that day was Tennants Creek, 400 miles away.

As the sun began to rise on our early start we witnessed the loveliest of sunrises, the sky a medley of every colour imaginable, as we sped on to Camooweal where we halted for breakfast. Just a one place hotel, where we had breakfast of steak and eggs, which I found difficult to tackle but before the day was out wished I had. It was late afternoon before we had the chance of getting any other refreshments. A good cup of tea with goats' milk was very welcome. Three miles out from Camooweal we crossed over the Queensland border into the Northern Territory, then continued through long stretches of barren land. The road was quite good as it had been constructed by the Americans during the 1939—1945 War, and kept in good repair. The bus was by no means comfortable, it being the mail bus and passengers its secondary consideration. Nevertheless it served its purpose, there being no other means of transport. We finally reached Tennants Creek at 6.30 p.m. It was hot and we were all very tired, though I guess it was nothing to what that poor driver suffered, he being the only one for that long, lone, dusty stretch.

Tennants Creek was once a gold-mining town, now obsolete. It has a very wide road with two hotels, one on either side, a few corrugated huts for shops, and a shortage of fresh water.

I spent only one night there, leaving next morning on the last lap of my journey to Alice Springs, 360 miles. The scenery was now becoming much more interesting. At a place spelt Wauchope, pronounced Walk-up, I was surprised to see the only spot of colour for almost a thousand miles, a tall oleander hedge surrounding the only house, full of pink blossom which must be a joy to the traveller. Somehow, someone had found sufficient water to keep that alive, although it did occur to me that they must have had an artesian well, as there are several throughout the outback.

For the next two miles we drove through what are known as the Devils Marbles, on either side of the road rock formations of all sizes and shapes, light brown in colour, and very smooth as though they had been subjected to the elements for many centuries, some weighing many tons. After a very pleasant journey I had at last reached Alice Springs, the place of my dreams! I stayed there at the Mount Gillen Hotel for a week. I simply loved 'the Alice' as the Australians call it, nestled in a hollow, surrounded by the MacDonnell Ranges, perhaps quite a different 'Alice' to when Neville Shute wrote about it. The wide bed of the Todd River goes through the town and was completely dry while I was there, though at times in the wet season it does run riot, when there is a lot of flooding, which may not be for many years in between. There are a variety of gum-trees along the river banks, ghost gums, silver, salmon, and blue gums. When their bark peels off the trunks, they are very attractive with their lovely colours. The ghost gums are really white and show up well in the dark, hence their name. All the trees seem to survive through drought and flood.

There are many places I would like to have explored outside the town, but the tours were much too expensive. One afternoon I went out to Simpsons Gap, not too far away. The bus took us along a rough bush track, through bumpy and dusty cattle country, though I failed to see what the poor animals lived on. During the dry season cattle are driven hundreds of miles to their watering-places, and there was evidence on every hand that many perished *en route*. Simpsons Gap is a pretty place with a creek running through gaps in the rock. The natural colouring of the rocks is quite unique. A grass meadow with gum-trees had a couple of drovers' hammocks slung between the branches. While there, we lit a fire and made true billycan tea, enjoyed by all. On our way to Simpsons Gap we passed the grave of the Reverend John Flynn. Known as 'Flynn of the Inland', Moderator of the Presbyterian Church, and founder of the Australian Inland Mission, and first Flying Doctor Service; he died in 1952, and requested that he be buried in the 'Outback' which he loved and served so well. So there he lies, with 'Mount Gillen' as it were keeping sentinel over him.

John Flynn certainly brought gladness and rejoicing to the wilderness and the solitary places, for from his first Pedal Radio has grown a vast network that reaches out to all the isolated regions of that vast lonely land.

A memorial church has now been built at Alice Springs in the grounds where the first Inland Mission Hospital was started. The bricks for the building were being made on the site while I was there by two Italians, and faced with pink and white marble quarried seventy miles out of Alice Springs. The church porch goes over a lily pond, and behind the church there was to be a John Flynn Museum with many of his possessions exhibited, such as his swag, billycan, and first pedal radio. John Flynn I believe did a lot of his early travels by camel. Now they are gone from the scene as far as travelling is concerned. While I was at Alice Springs I visited the Flying Doctor Base, and heard messages being transmitted, and received from all over Australia, which was very interesting.

Another day I went to a private house to see a lovely opal collection. It was from this collection that the stone was chosen for Her Majesty's presentation brooch during her visit.

Then one day, wandering on my own, I came across the prison, only very small. The warden and his wife were enjoying a break outside their little house, surrounded by orange trees. They invited me to sit with them over a cup of tea and chat. They were a very nice, friendly couple.

When I left Alice Springs to return to Tennants Creek, as the bus left the town, we were followed on either side by lots of the big red kangaroos hopping along, having been disturbed in their early morning quest for food. It was wonderful to see such animals at close range. Another night was spent at the same hotel at Tennants Creek, starting off next morning for Darwin, going right through the middle of the northern outback, through Daly Waters, Katherine, Adelaide River, almost another 1,000 miles, breaking our journey for the night at Daly Waters.

We arrived at sunset just as a flock of pink and grey galahs were settling down to roost in a nearby tree. It was a lovely sight, with the rosy glow of the setting sun lighting up their plumage. From Daly Waters we continued right through to Darwin, which has been rebuilt since I was there. I only remember seeing the hospital and one hotel. On my travels I talked with a number of people, and learnt a lot. One lady suggested I tried 'The Country Women's Association' to stay at in Darwin, which I did, by telephone booking on arrival. They only took four visitors, but they had a vacancy, so I took a taxi to the house, where I stayed for three days before I set off by boat from Darwin, to go all round the north-west coast to Fremantle.

The boat was called *'Kabbarli'*, Aborigine for Little Grandmother. This boat was built by the State Shipping Company of Western Australia in memory of Daisy Bates who died in 1951, at the grand old age of 92 years, having spent most of her lifetime improving conditions for the Aboriginal people. What a lovely gesture on the part of the West Australian Government to have honoured her name in that way. The *Kabbarli* took a fortnight to reach Fremantle, and a very interesting trip it was. We called at several places to load and unload cargo — Wyndham, Port Sampson, Broom, Onslow, and Carnarvon. At Wyndham there was a large meat works. The main street was lined by an avenue of bottle-trees, which I would not have missed for anything. Their great trunks were shaped like huge bottles which seemed indestructible.

Port Sampson was the prettiest. The headland was covered with wild sturt peas, large pinky-red flowers, with black centres. At Onslow, wool was being loaded, pressed and packed into large square Hessian bales. At Carnarvon we went over the whaling station, which was very interesting but horribly smelly. Then out to an experimental fruit farm, and in another section I saw for the first time, cotton growing on bushes, bursting out of pods. Without stopping at Geraldton we proceeded to Fremantle.

I spent a month back in Perth renewing friendships from my previous visit, and managed to get to Albany Bay, 200 miles from Perth to visit the mother of a friend of mine living in England. It was winter by then, wet and windy, so I did not see Albany at its best. It has the most beautiful natural harbour.

Returning to Perth, I then left by train to return to the Eastern States, through Kalgooli, once the chief gold-mining centre of the west. There I changed trains and took the Trans-Australian air-conditioned train with an observation lounge, which took me across the Nullabor Plain, 300 miles of single straight railway line, taking two and a half days.

The train stopped at several places to leave goods for the scattered Aborigine families, and to pick up any passengers wanting to travel on the line to South Australia. The landscape all the way was a veritable waste of unproductive scrub land until we reached civilisation at Port Augusta, Port Pirri and Adelaide, for me only a short stay, but I did manage a coach tour, high up in the hills to Mount Lofty, which has wonderful views all over Adelaide.

The next evening I was off on the night train to Melbourne. On this particular train you booked a Roomette, the whole train consisting of separate compartments, self-contained, and carpeted throughout. On opening a sliding door there was an easy chair. Looking like a cupboard in the wall is your bed. You just release a spring and the bed comes down, already made up, with an inner sprung mattress and white sheets, two pillows, and pale blue pure wool blankets. It also had a flush toilet, hot and cold running water, several mirrors with lights over each, an electric plug for a gentleman's shaver, waste-paper basket, and a shoe box which opened from the passage, should you wish to have your shoes cleaned. Early morning tea and biscuits, with the local paper, was delivered to each roomette. You would be amazed to see the small space all these gadgets were tucked into.

The train arrived at Melbourne at 9 a.m. There I was met by an English couple who were on the Barrier Reef cruise with me. They lived at Sale in Gippsland, Victoria, 100 miles from Melbourne. They had come by car so I had a lovely drive back with them, and stayed a week. Their home and surroundings were typically English, a bungalow with two meadows, a house cow, chickens, etc. All very peaceful. Their family were married, living nearby. I went to several interesting places, and one day to Lakes Entrance, where several rivers merge to join forces on their way to the sea. There was also a ninety-mile coastline of golden sand.

Returning to Melbourne by train I stayed at The People's Palace, an hotel managed by the Salvation Army, where I allowed myself plenty of time to explore. One day I did a coach tour to the Danderong Ranges up in the hills. We stopped for morning tea, as the Australians call it, at a very nice house at the foot of the Ranges, opposite cherry orchards. They reminded me of a verse by Joseph Addison, who said: 'I value my garden more for being full of blackbirds, than of cherries. And very frankly give them fruit, for their song.'

The tour through the Ranges took us along several miles of wooded countryside and fern-lined tracks, passing on our way 3,000 feet up, a picturesque church of local stone, built for a lady as a memorial to her husband. From the top of the Ranges one had a magnificent view of the whole of Melbourne.

My stay in Australia was coming to an end. I had been there over two years, and was now leaving Melbourne for Sydney to spend my last two weeks with friends at their flat before going on to New Zealand, where I had already obtained a position in a maternity hospital at New Plymouth. We made the most of our time together. Over the weekend we went by car to Katoomba, sixty miles north of Sydney, a National Park in the Blue Mountains. Then on through Bathurst and Orange, where we stayed overnight. Then back by way of another scenic drive. I said farewell to Australia on 19th August 1954, sad to be leaving that beautiful country which I had come to love, its wealth of beauty, flora and fauna, the outback, and bush country with an atmosphere all its own. But by no means least, the Australian people themselves, who had shown me so much kindness and hospitality. All the nurses I had worked with in complete harmony, and the happy times we had together. My friends saw me off by boat to Wellington, their usual method of saying farewell being festoons of multi-coloured streamers decked all over the boat. Then as I was about to board, a parting gift of a toy koala was given to me, which I still have and treasure.

August 1954 found me on my way to New Zealand. The boat trip to Wellington was most enjoyable, calm seas all the way. My first impression of New Zealand was marred by the fact that it was raining heavily, with mist shrouding the hills around the town. I had arranged to stay in Wellington that night, so when the mist cleared I was able to see what Wellington looked like. There were some very fine buildings, and a coast road of several miles around newly-built estates. The next morning I set off by bus for New Plymouth, a journey of just over 200 miles. The countryside was very green after the winter rains. Now spring was on its way with spring flowers opening up everywhere, and hundreds of lambs in the fields. Mount Egmont is only sixteen miles from New Plymouth, so as we approached we had a wonderful view of it, rising to a height of over 8,000 feet. New Plymouth is quite a small township, on the west coast, midway between Wellington and Auckland. The beaches have black sand, not that anyone would get dirty handling it, but due to the many minerals it contains. There are also the attractive Sugar Loaf Rocks, jutting out into the sea.

The Maternity Hospital where I worked was an annex of the big General Hospital, called 'Ahura', probably a Maori name. It was not very large but was always busy. It was a few minutes walk from the main building, so all the staff lived in the cottage next door, the matron having a nice little cottage of her own, with her two cats. And she had a ladder made for them, so that they could come and go as they wished from her sitting-room to the garden. They always used it. I was pleased to be back with mothers and babies once more. I earned a lot more money in Australia than England, and even more in New Zealand. We only had one day off a week, but all the places were too far afield to get to in one day, so I saved hard to do all my sightseeing in one big swoop before leaving for England. I was determined to get to the South Island as I had been told all the real beauty was to be found there, though to me it was all beautiful.

There were some beautiful parks in New Plymouth, 'Pukakura' was the gem. Then there was Churchill Heights, a smaller one, from which one could see for miles around. We had a perfectly lovely summer, apparently quite the best for a number of years. Needless to say rain was badly needed everywhere. While I was at New Plymouth, I was sent out to a Maternity Hospital at Waitara, ten miles out of town, to relieve the Maori sister for her holiday. It was a modern hospital, built especially for the Maori people, to encourage them to have their babies in sanitary conditions. The Maoris are a very nice race of people, and their babies are adorable, with their big brown eyes, masses of brown hair, and placid temperaments. I used to love bathing them, and setting their lovely hair into waves. I stayed seven months at New Plymouth, and saved £200 for my boat fare home, which I booked before leaving. I had promised friends that I would be back home for their Golden Wedding in July 1955. Just imagine, I was able to travel over 12,000 miles for £200, doing it in first-class luxury. In the fifties, their money was sterling, but now for many years has been in dollars.

I left New Plymouth on 7th March, and stopped off at Waitomo on my way to Auckland, spending two nights at the Waitomo Caves Hotel. During the evening we were taken on a conducted tour of the glorious Waitomo Caves, housing in their numerous crevices thousands of glow-worms. An underground river meanders through the caves, so we went for a short distance along its banks in a rowing boat. All the lights in the caves were extinguished, and we were told not to speak. The picture that confronted us was truly magnificent, for all the world as though a myriad twinkling stars were shining down on us, from the tails of these glow-worms.

The next afternoon I continued my journey by bus to Auckland, where I stayed ten days, during which I did a lot of sightseeing of the city and suburbs. There were some panoramic views from the top of Mount Eden. Auckland has a beautiful harbour. It could easily be a miniature Sydney with its beautiful bridge, and many beaches surrounding the harbour. Leaving Auckland I went much further north to Whangarei, where I changed buses for Russell, and The Bay of Islands. The previous day they had had a tropical downpour from 10 a.m. to 4 p.m., thus breaking a six months' drought, resulting in some serious flooding.

Our bus to Russell had to make a seven-mile detour to dodge the floods along the main road. Even then we ploughed through a lot of flood water. The journey was really lovely, up and down winding narrow roads, through gorges and native bush, coming out at intervals upon little Maori homesteads. The bus passing through appeared to be the event of the day. The entire family gathered, complete with their horses, and numerous dogs, with an occasional cat viewing the situation from the top of a bank. Father seemed to be the favourite with the children, for wherever he alighted there was great excitement, with the tiny tots, dancing and skipping all the way up to the house. Maybe father had something in his pocket from the big town. Owing to the floods we were two hours late arriving at our guest-house. The evening meal was well and truly over, but they did find us something of a sort.

After breakfast the next morning I joined a party going out by launch to The Bay of Islands, from where the first missionary settlement was established in 1814. It was a nice sunny morning, but cold on the water. There are many small islands out in the bay, full of history and legend which were described to us as we went along. We went ashore on one of the larger islands for lunch. No sooner had we settled down to enjoy our sandwiches, then flocks of seagulls appeared, demanding we share our lunch with them. On our last evening at the guest-house we wandered down to the end of the jetty to watch the fishing boats return. There was always a competition as to who would bring in the largest fish, which were weighed on huge scales at the end of the jetty. Great excitement. Unless I had seen it all, I would never have believed there were such great fish in the sea. It took three men to hook one up onto the scales.

Leaving Russell I retraced my steps to Auckland for another night, setting off the next day for Rotorua, a veritable wonderland with its thermal activity, boiling mud pools, fenced off, which really bubbled. Plop! Plop! Not to mention the geysers which at intervals spurted many feet into the air. I stayed at a small family hotel with a nice garden. They had their own mineral pool indoors, which was very relaxing. Nearly all the houses are able to cook by conserved heat from the hot springs. On the edges of the pools, local people were cooking their vegetables tied up in cotton bags.

One afternoon I went out to the Blue and Green Lakes and wandered round the ruins of the buried village which succumbed to the 1886 volcanic eruption. Another day I visited the Fairy and Rainbow Springs with their attractive trout pools. Leaving for Wellington, I went by way of the desert road, motoring for many miles along the shores of Lake Taupo, and so back to Wellington for one night, before leaving for a quick tour of the South Island.

In glorious sunshine and a calm sea I went by boat to Picton in the South Island, through the Marlborough, and the beautiful Queen Charlotte Sound, high rugged mountains, with isolated homesteads nestling on the water's edge. I almost envied their quiet mode of life. Arriving at Picton, the bus was waiting to take passengers on to Nelson, where we arrived at 10 p.m. Nelson is a pretty little place, famous for its apple orchards, and the growing of hops and tobacco. It also has the reputation of being the sunniest spot in the whole of New Zealand. It certainly lived up to it while I was there.

After a stay of three days I proceeded down the West Coast through Murchison to West Port, and then for seventy miles along the scenic coast road, with its Pancake Rocks to Greymouth, which is typical of its name. A ghost gold-mining town, it later resorted to coal-mining. Just passing through, then on to Hokitika and Ross, to the Franz Joseph and Fox Glaciers. We did not stay long at Franz Joseph as the hotel had been burnt down the previous year, so there was only a small motor camp. We then went on to the Fox Hotel where I stayed three days. The following morning I went with a party that was going onto the glacier itself. We had to put on thick woollen socks and hobnail boots. Then we went by car along a bush track for two miles before starting off for the glacier itself. Clambering and climbing over huge boulders of rock, and across pools of water, before finally getting onto the glacier.

It was very hard going, and on a couple of occasions I thought I would have to abandon it, but when I saw the wonders of nature spread out before me, I was glad I had made the effort. The glacier is nine miles long, surrounded by high mountain ranges, with numerous waterfalls joining to swell a raging river beneath. The formations of the ice caves were unbelievable. We were able to walk right through one of them, and out the other side. From The Fox, I was hoping to have got through to Queenstown, but discovered there was no road, so had to retrace my steps to Hokitika, from where I went by train right across the island, crossing the Southern Alps, and the Canterbury Plains, with a wonderful view of Mount Cook from the train, and finally to Christchurch, which is considered the typical English city. The River Avon wends its way through the town, with lots of weeping willows along its banks, swans on the river, with a view of Christchurch Cathedral. All very similar to our Stratford-upon-Avon in Warwickshire.

From Christchurch I went to Dunedin, the Scottish settlement, then down to Invercargill in the extreme south of the island, and inland to Queenstown, the gem of the South Island, on the banks of Lake Whakatipu, surrounded by mountain ranges, aptly named 'The Remarkables'. There I came across a very nice park in which there was a fine memorial of Captain Scott and his companions who set off from New Zealand on that hazardous journey to the South Pole on 26th November 1910, in that little wooden ship, the *Terra Nova*, with its yellow painted funnel. Sadly only four of that brave party made it back home. I left the park, which was looking beautiful, with the many poplars all in their glorious autumn colours, and the mountain ranges, already snow-capped.

Reluctantly after two days I had to be on my way again, back to Christchurch to leave on the night boat from the Port of Llyttelton, for Wellington, where I spent another three days before embarking for home on 14th April 1955. Our liner was the largest of the New Zealand Shipping Company. The *Rangitani* was very nice and comfortable and beautifully furnished. I had a first-class single cabin complete with a full-sized bathroom. It was quite the last word in luxury, which I was making the most of, not expecting ever to travel in such style again. Now unfortunately there are no passenger liners. The air services have put paid to those, which is a pity for the few who wish to travel at leisure.

For the first few days out from Wellington the weather was cold and stormy, but improved as we went along. By the time we reached Panama it was sweltering. The crew were out in their white uniforms, and passengers were in sun suits and shorts, the swimming-pool being the main attraction. Our first stop was Pitcairn Island, arriving at 4 a.m., to allow the islanders on board to sell their wares. All the passengers were up bright and early. It was a lovely starlit morning just before daybreak. It was a unique sight to see their four large boats painted white, filled to capacity with both young and old, men and women, heavily laden, glide alongside our large ship. As soon as they had manoeuvred their boats and tied them together, they climbed up two long rope ladders with their heavy bags, as nimble as mountain goats. Mostly their goods consisted of well-made shopping and sewing baskets, fans, beads, carved wooden flying fish, but even more popular was their fruit. Large ripe bananas, eight a shilling. Juicy sweet oranges five a shilling, and pawpaws, which sold like hot cakes. The islanders were very nice people, nearly all speaking good English.

Pitcairn Island from our ship looked like a large green hill, but is in fact two miles long and one mile wide, and rises to a height of over a thousand feet above sea level. There were about 140 people living on the island. When time was up, which amounted to about three hours, the ship's siren sounded, and in no time they were packed up and away down those dangerous-looking ladders. As soon as they had got their boats clear of our swell, they put up their sails and glided back to their island home, the rising sun lighting up the way before them. It was an unforgettable sight, and certainly worth getting up early to witness.

Pitcairn Island will be better known for its association with the Mutiny on *The Bounty*. By 1800 the only surviving mutineer was John Adams, then thirty-six years of age. He became a Christian and with the aid of a Bible and a Prayer Book saved from *The Bounty* taught the young and growing community to read and write. John Adams survived until 1829, having spent thirty-nine years on the island. In 1808 a passing vessel discovered the island to be inhabited, and news of the small community reached England for the first time. Thirty years later Pitcairn was annexed to the Crown. By 1856 the population had swelled to 193, which was more than the island could support, and so the British Government moved some of them to Norfolk Island. Within two years however, many grew homesick and returned to Pitcairn, and it is the 200 odd descendants of these who inhabit the island today.

Our next stop was Panama where we arrived just as it was getting dark. What a pity we were unable to see it in daylight. However, we had a coach trip around Panama and the suburbs, ending up at the hotel which was very luxurious. It had its own row of shops, a large circular dance floor in the middle of a palm grove, and a swimming-pool. I did not go into the hotel. It was so hot everywhere I was glad to get back to our air-conditioned boat. We left Panama at 6 a.m. the following morning to go through the Panama Canal, which took roughly nine hours. The Canal is a most wonderful feat of engineering, with the brains behind the planning of it, the hard work and much loss of life during the building of it. All this I thought about as I stood on deck watching the large ship being lowered and raised into position through the different locks. It was a truly wonderful experience and a privilege to have been able to witness and enjoy it all.

The Canal that was opened to the world's traffic on 15th August 1914, is fifty miles in length. Approaching the Canal from the Caribbean Sea a vessel enters Limon Bay and proceeds seven miles up the channel to Gatun Locks, where she is raised eighty-five feet through a triple series of locks to the level of Gatun Lake. Then for twenty-five miles, full speed can be maintained to Gamboa at the head of the reach, where the lake merges into the famous Gaillard Cut, nine miles in length. Here the greatest of the excavations of all were made, and on the left bank is Gold Hill, 660 feet above sea-level, which was the scene of severe landslides in the early days of the Canal. The Gaillard Cut ends at Pedro Miguel Locks where vessels are lowered twenty-seven feet to the level of the Miraflores Lake, where in two further stages ships are lowered the remaining fifty-eight feet to sea-level, from the Miraflores Locks. Three days out from Panama we arrived at the Dutch Colony of Curacao. Willemstad the capital bears a vivid resemblance to Holland with its quaint 17th century architecture. The whole character of the town, and of the whole island, has been undergoing considerable change since the advent of the oil refinery industry in 1916.

E

The open fruit market down on the water's edge was very picturesque. All the fruit for sale was brought up from the boats.

That was our last stop. We then only had another three days' journey to Southampton. My friends came from Plymouth by car to meet me. It was lovely seeing them again and travelling back to Devon in springtime, with all the fresh green leaves on the trees, spring flowers, and bird-song. To me, England is home, and however far I may roam, I would always want to be coming back.

PART SIX   1955—1970

Whatsoever things are,
True, Honest, Just, Pure, Lovely.
Whatsoever things are of good report.
If there be any virtue,
and if there be any Praise,
Think on these things.
Philippians 4. v.8.

Returning home was wonderful and I had plenty to talk about. Friends kindly let me have a room in their house until I was able to find work and somewhere to live.

First of all I bought a *Nursing Mirror* to see what nursing vacancies were on offer. Almost the first I saw was a District Midwife required by Plymouth Corporation, so I had no need to look any further. I applied for the vacancy, and was asked to go for an interview and was appointed to start in June 1955, just two weeks later. At the interview I was asked if I could drive a car, that being essential for my work. Never having driven one since 1947 when working in Norfolk, I didn't possess a car, but that was not going to stop me from buying one, and taking a driving test which by then was compulsory.

I bought a new spruce-green Austin A30, only £400 then. I was quite excited. "The Ultimate" — a car of my very own.

I then thought I ought to have a few driving lessons and learn something about the Highway Code. I enjoyed my first lesson as there was a car on view to instruct us about what was under the bonnet, and also how to change a tyre. The next week I went out with an instructor who didn't seem at all interested in his job, and had the same one the following week, but before the lesson was over he said, 'You will never drive a car', to which I replied, 'Not with you sitting beside me'.

So that was the end of my driving lessons, but not the end of driving.

There was a disused airstrip on Dartmoor which a friend offered to take me to, using my own car, so I was able to get in quite a lot of practice. A few weeks later I was booked to take my driving test. We didn't have to wait so long in those days as the roads were not so cluttered up with as many cars. My test started and finished at Devonport Barracks. To my delight I passed first time. So now I was in order to get on with the work appointed to me.

I knew district midwifery would be hard work, but I much preferred that to working in hospitals.

The friends' Golden Wedding that I had come home for was in July. It was a very happy day with a tea-party at their home, to which many friends were invited.

Several months elapsed before I was able to have my own home. A new flat was allotted me by Plymouth Council. It was well out of town on Austin Farm Estate near Egg Buckland village, a pretty little place with a beautiful old church. I believe the name of the village means Church in Deerland. It was lovely countryside in the Forder Valley, now completely ruined with thousands of houses and industrial estates, built all over that beautiful farming countryside.

My flat was high up with a lovely view; a field on the opposite side of the road with a stream running through the valley. How I enjoyed buying my furniture, carpets, making curtains and setting up my very first home where I lived happily for over fifteen years, bringing me up to my retirement. My rent for the flat, plus garage, was deducted each month from my salary before I got it, leaving me very little to live on.

There was a nice piece of garden at the front which I kept gay with flowers in spring and summer. At the rear a much larger plot on a steep slope was difficult to cope with, though I did manage to grow nearly all my own vegetables.

Each year many gypsy families invaded the field opposite. One year I counted twenty-one caravans, each with their dogs, cats and chickens. One year a very young donkey was included, who woke up the whole estate at the crack of dawn with his repeated loud 'Hee-Haws'! A lot of the people objected to the gypsies, but I quite looked forward to the event. Their animals were never a nuisance. The dogs, greyhounds, which I suspect were used for racing, never moved away from the families who owned them. The chickens were in netted enclosures which were moved along daily to different parts of the field. Cats, which I adore, will go their own sweet way, doing exactly as they like.

As soon as the caravans arrived everything was taken out for a good clean-up, and clothes-lines rigged up to dry their washing. There were many visits to the site by local police as they were not really allowed on the land. Periodically they got moved on. Eventually the Council built a permanent camp for them on a secluded piece of ground, but that was not their way of living, always wanting to be on the move. Later the camp was deserted and a hazard to the young people in the district, so it was finally demolished.

The whole of that area has since seen a great change. New roads and bridges have been built to carry the ever-increasing traffic over the Tamar Bridge into Cornwall.

Needless to say I very much enjoyed my work as a district midwife. It was a very hectic life with a lot of responsibility, which I seemed to thrive on. We all had a large area to cover. The midwives adjoining each other's areas also relieved each other for their days off, and all holidays. It was very tiring at times, often being up all night and working all day. We also had lots of home visits, and clinics to do; all bookings of anyone on our particular patch who wanted to have their babies at home. It was very satisfying work as we got to know all our mothers and their families well long before their babies were born, on several occasions there being four in the same family, which was very rewarding.

After settling into my flat I was able to have pets of my own; Bobby the budgerigar was the first, given to me by a grateful father who bred them himself in a lovely aviary adjoining his house. He let me choose the one I would like, a blue and grey male. He soon learned to talk and was great company for over ten years.

A year or two later a friend who lived on a farm phoned to say she was getting rid of all her cats, and would I have the only one left. I couldn't bear the thought of it having to die, so the next day I went to the farm on Roborough Downs, Dartmoor, to collect him. He was a thin little black and white kitten, only a few weeks old, not a bit handsome, but a great lovable character. I put him in a box, but before I was out of the drive he had escaped from that and climbed onto the back seat, where he sat looking out of the window all the way home. At traffic lights he was spotted by many motorists who were quite amused by him. When I arrived home my neighbour was outside with Johnnie, her lovely brown spaniel dog, and wanted to know what I had got and what I was going to name him, then said, 'Why don't you call him Toby?' So Toby he became. I put him down beside Johnnie and they seemed to become friends right away. He was a great pet, always around when he heard my car coming down the road, running down the steps to sit on the wall at the bottom. He also knew who liked him. One year I had a friend to stay who couldn't stand cats. Poor Toby spent most of the two weeks sitting on top of the garden shed.

One day when I was called out to a case, I inadvertently left the sitting-room door open, which I always made a point of closing as I never trusted Toby alone with the bird. When I returned several hours later I found that Toby had knocked over the cage which was on a stand. The glass was all broken, mixed up with bird seed and water. Bobby was still in his cage unhurt. Toby was hiding away in his sleeping box in the kitchen, afraid to come out and face me.

Driving home after a night case in the early morning, which I considered to be the best part of the day, often had its compensations. One morning as it was beginning to get light, I saw a fox crossing Forder Valley Road on his way home from a night's foraging. Another time I spotted a badger coming out of a field into a country lane. Then one spring morning, after being shut up all night in a prefab, as I left, a cuckoo flew low overhead with his loud 'cu-choo'!, settling in a tree a few feet away, no doubt to deposit her egg in another bird's nest, to hatch, feed and bring up her offspring.

Several times I spotted the same white owl sitting on top of a hedge. The wood-pigeon may be the first to make his voice heard in the countryside, but I vote the blackbird to be the most industrious, who I would always see, scattering the fallen leaves at the sides of the country lanes to find his early breakfast.

The grey squirrels also gave me much pleasure, racing across the road and darting up the trees on the other side. Not to forget when it was really dark, many a cat whose shining eyes I could pick out in the car headlights.

There were two amusing animal incidents. At one house, a Siamese cat who rushed upstairs making a terribly noisy complaint, objecting to the smell of Dettol! Another night a lady was having her baby downstairs so as not to disturb her other children. She had her budgerigar in the corner of the room with the cage covered over. As soon as the baby boy was born and gave his first loud cry, the budgie responded by ringing his bell vigorously. What a joy that was.

And so the years quickly passed on into the 1960s. I was beginning to feel very tired and thought it was old age creeping on, or possibly the demanding work taking its toll. I carried on as long as I could until one day I came to a complete full stop, unable to walk more than a few steps.

After almost a month in hospital for bone marrow and blood tests etc., not being able to have any treatment until the test results were known, I was diagnosed as having pernicious anaemia, the last thing I had thought about. What a blessing I developed it when I did, for it was not until after the war that treatment had been found for it. I can remember when I was doing my general nursing training there was just nothing that could be done for these patients. There is no actual cure, but as long as one continues treatment to the end of their days, they can live an active life.

From the word go I have given my own treatment, being well for over twenty years now. It saves a lot of wasted time in doctors' waiting-rooms. I thank God daily for my threescore years and ten, and count any extra as a bonus, including discovered treatment.

I was off duty for about three months and had a good rest.

When I was able to drive my car again, my first outing was over the Tamar Bridge into Cornwall, to 'Cotehele House', National Trust property, near Calstock, beside the River Tamar. There I spent an enjoyable afternoon, and a short walk in the gardens. Before I went back on duty I spent a week with friends at a small hotel overlooking the sea at St. Ives, Cornwall.

When I was in hospital, nursing standards had already fallen to their lowest ebb, long before this government came into being. I should know for I was caught up in it. As a patient I was absolutely horrified at what went on, and what was not done. At that time there was a free-for-all visiting time in operation. Visitors even with their children were allowed in at any time of the day. It was absolute bedlam. I could have done with the single room that was vacant as I was in need of some rest and quiet. Instead I was at one end of a thirty-bedded ward with bathrooms at the other end which I hadn't the strength to walk to. The help I got was from other patients who were recovering and able to get about.

We hardly ever saw a nurse in the ward. The ward orderlies were very kind and did more for us than any of the nursing staff. The Sister-in-Charge had to walk the length of the ward to get to her office at the far end, but never once did I hear her say a 'good morning' or even look at a patient as she walked past. I thought that was just awful.

However, I continued to enjoy my last few years as a district midwife, and was sad to retire at sixty. If only I had been allowed to see my last few mothers that I had booked through their confinements, I would have retired feeling satisfied, not as it then seemed to me, an unfinished chapter.

PART SEVEN

Not what we have but what we use,
Not what we see but what we choose.
These are the things that mar and bless
The sum of Human happiness.
Anon

My first free day left me no time for brooding. Three friends arrived from Australia to stay for a few days. What with preparing extra meals and organising visits to places of interest, our days were full and enjoyable. We explored Plymouth, The Hoe, Dartmoor, Princetown, and had a lovely drive all around Burrator Reservoir on the outskirts of Dartmoor through wooded countryside with distant views of the many granite tors, all individually named.

Our next tour was over the Tamar Bridge into Cornwall, taking the Truro road to have a look at the town and cathedral, then onto the Penzance road through Redruth and Camborne, with many reminders of the old tin-mining days, the brick chimney-stack ruins standing out all over the landscape. A few miles short of Penzance, I turned onto the coast road to visit the picturesque town of Marazion with its beautiful view of St. Michael's Mount, a small island out in Mounts Bay rising 230ft above sea-level; a lovely walk along the causeway when the tide is out, and by ferry boat when the tide is in.

The island is steeped in history. Tradition claims that the Christian religion was established on The Mount in the fifth century. The castle is opened to the public on certain days during the summer months. At one time it was the residence of Lord and Lady St. Leven, and with the Mount, in possession of the St. Aubyn family from about 1657—1954, when Lord St. Leven transferred it to the National Trust. At the top of the Mount is a lovely little church which is still used for Sunday morning worship, but it is a very steep climb up a rocky path to get there. The church can only take a congregation of sixty-five, who have to produce admission tickets to the service.

Now on to Penzance for a wander round the town, and then to Land's End through several miles of country roads before getting back to the coast, where suddenly one is confronted with a glorious view of the rugged coastline out to the Longships Lighthouse, in the Atlantic Ocean. You could happily spend days at Land's End. There is so much to see, and there are many beautiful walks around the coast, much of it now owned by the National Trust. When at all possible I never missed driving over the moors, with nature at its very best, and often found my way back to Plymouth over Bodmin Moor through St. Austell, into the china clay country, the huge mountains of white clay resembling snow-covered mountains. Now, when the pits are worked out, they are landscaped so that they eventually become covered with chalk-loving shrubs and plants.

One day we had a lovely drive through parts of North Devon and Exmoor, and on their last day, a picnic tea on Dartmoor, among the flowering heathers, grazing sheep and Dartmoor ponies.

Now it was back to reality as I knew I would have to leave my flat which had been my first home for over fifteen years, to be handed over to another midwife. I had no idea how difficult it was going to be finding unfurnished accommodation. Unless one has enough money to buy a home, there is just nothing else.

Eventually I managed to get temporary accommodation in Kingsbridge, a place I knew well, a pretty, quaint old town with a very steep main street running down to a quay alongside a sheltered creek, surrounded by some of the loveliest countryside anywhere in South Devon. Before leaving Plymouth I knew I could not expect a very good pension as I had broken my service when I emigrated to Australia. Plymouth Corporation wanted to know the addresses of all the places I had worked at in Australia, Tasmania, and New Zealand before they could assess the pension I was entitled to, which worked out at £208 a year, and my retirement pension £6 a week.

The Nurses' Pension is Index Linked, so I am now a lot better off. We get an increase at the beginning of each financial year, which varies considerably. One year I got an extra £12 increase, then the Income Tax people deducted an extra £1 a month. So where was I? No better off! Fortunately money never worries me as I have only ever had what I worked for, and never bought anything until I had the amount saved for what I needed.

I had to buy three cars during the time I was doing district midwifery. We were never supplied with them, and it was only a year or two before I retired that we were given a car allowance, which did not cover the cost of petrol, let alone tyres, repairs, insurance, road fund licence, etc. New cars were very cheap then. After parting with my Austin A30, I had two Austin A40s. The Farina models were lovely cars and very reliable; they only cost £600—£800, but would be thousands now. Sadly that model went out of production.

I am very disappointed how some of the nurses are letting their profession down — out on the streets with banners and plastic buckets demanding more money. I know things are much more expensive, but do they know they are paid more a week than I got in a year? After qualifying as a psychiatric nurse, my monthly pay was less than £4.00 a month. But living in our Nurses' Home with three meals a day was a great help. Then when I went to a voluntary hospital to do my SRN training I had even less. Thinking back I often wonder how I ever managed to keep myself in shoes and stockings.

During the war years we could not go anywhere, so that saved us spending the little we had. Quite honestly I never heard our nurses talk about money. We just accepted what we were given. We were happy, being able to help people through our work. Find out what God would have you do and do it well. Who was it said: 'The noblest minds the best contentment have'? We would need to be saints to get into that category, but it is worth thinking about. *Where has all the dedication gone?* I would like to see matrons back again in charge of the hospitals as they were in my day. There are now far too many administrators, and not enough workers. How much more satisfying to be doing the actual practical work.

There were no antibiotics during my training. Our patients recovered through sheer good nursing. After leaving school I only tolerated the work I had to do as I had no other option, until I could work out something better for myself. Even when I emigrated to Australia, within forty-eight hours of landing at Fremantle, West Australia, I knew it was going to be a case of 'God helps those who help themselves', as I had to find all my own work.

I have often been asked why I never married. Being caught between two wars was in itself a stumbling block, all the young men of my age group going off to war. I remember once telling a friend if I wasn't married by the time I was twenty-four I would never marry. Somehow marriage never really appealed to me, especially after I started nursing I knew I had found my niche in life.

I am by nature a loner, as I never knew any love during my childhood. Although I made a lot of friends through nursing, friendship and family ties, come into different categories.

Living in Kingsbridge finding work was difficult to come by, which for me was imperative. The small amount of money coming in weekly was not going to pay my rent, etc. There was a Cottage Hospital in Kingsbridge, but by government orders they were not allowed to employ any retired nurses on pension. However, I got to hear about an elderly lady who needed some help, and between times motored out to Ashprington, a lovely little village near Totnes, to take an elderly couple out in my car twice a week to do their shopping. Eventually I got a post in a private nursing home in Torquay, owned by a group of private doctors. There I settled down and when the matron retired I was asked if I would take over on a temporary basis, which I did until that home closed down, to reopen in another part of Torquay.

Toby, my cat, came to Kingsbridge with me and then to Torquay. I could take him anywhere. The ladies at the nursing home loved him. One in particular, who had a ground-floor room, would leave her window open so that he could get in. She always liked an afternoon nap, so if Toby was missing I always knew where to find him — curled up on the bed beside her. I had Toby for sixteen years and was heartbroken when he died about three years after I moved to Cornwall.

I had found a warden's post with accommodation in a beautiful village in Cornwall on the Roseland Peninsula — a cluster of almshouses, consisting of four bungalows and two round houses. I had a little house to myself in a lovely garden. We were quite near the sea at Portscatho — the name of the village was St. Just-in-Roseland, a beautiful unique village which should never be missed on the way to St. Mawes. The castle at St. Mawes has been restored and made into a museum. Each year our church held their annual garden party and sale of goods in the museum grounds on the edge of the cliffs, a lovely spot overlooking Falmouth Bay, with Pendennis Castle across the water high up on the opposite headland. There were so many lovely places to visit that I often went out exploring during an afternoon.

After three years at the Homes, I thought I would retire for good, if I could find somewhere to live. Through asking around I heard that there was an empty farm cottage in the area, and got in touch with the people who owned it. They said they would have to think about it. Weeks slipped by and after several enquiries I eventually got it to rent, and had it redecorated inside before I moved in. I bought some flower tubs to put along the cottage wall leading to the front door to brighten up the place, with lots of lovely spring flowers early in the year, then begonias and bedding annuals in the summer. I also made a rose garden in the front, and grew vegetables and soft fruits — strawberries, raspberries, blackcurrants and gooseberries — in the back garden. There is no better therapy than a couple of hours working in the garden to dispel 'the blues'. As that lovely poem, 'The Glory of the Garden' states: 'One is nearer God's heart in a garden than anywhere else on earth.'

As soon as I moved into the cottage, one of the farm cats, 'Tamsie', appeared and took over. She always went out at night as there were plenty of warm sheds with hay to curl up in, but was always at the door in the morning for her breakfast. Periodically she would bring in a kitten when they were big enough and needed extra food. They soon became tame. They were such pretty little kittens; I would love to have kept the lot, instead they were all found good homes.

I loved living at the cottage. It was so quiet and peaceful. On a balmy summer's evening it was wonderful to stand outside and listen to the stillness. There is always music among the trees in the garden, but our hearts must be very quiet to hear it. My cottage was surrounded by fields with grazing cattle. I loved to hear the cows wending their way along the lane at milking time. There were some wonderful views from my bedroom window of all that was going on around the farms in the vicinity.

One very cold, frosty morning, I witnessed twin calves being born in the field adjoining the cottage. I phoned the farmer who came and carried them into a nice warm barn, mother bringing up the rear. The field was too slippery for the new arrivals to manage.

Then when the drought of 1976 came, there was no rain for many weeks, not a vestige of green anywhere. All the fields were dried up. A family of partridges appeared, the parents with a family of seven chicks. Every evening they would bring them into the field when it was getting cooler, when there would be lots of flies for them to feed on.

You would hardly think that anything could grow in such dry conditions but suddenly the fields were full of mushrooms growing in profusion. There must have been thousands, all edible ones. I love field mushrooms, but all the gates leading into the fields were securely tied up to keep out trespassers, so I never had any. The cultivated ones never taste as good as the ones we personally pluck out of the fields heavy with dew in the early mornings. Also that year there was a bumper crop of blackberries everywhere.

Finding work seemed to have become a habit of mine. Every Monday morning I used to go into Truro to work for a lady, and two afternoons a week from 2—8 p.m. to help at a

Convent Nursing Home, run by the nuns, which I enjoyed very much. It was a lovely drive, twelve miles each way.

One year we had a very cold wintry spell when we were cut off from civilisation for several weeks by huge snow-drifts. The milk tanker was unable to get through to collect the farmer's milk, and there was no electricity or telephones working. I happened to have a gas picnic stove which came in handy, and coal for the fires. But I never knew when the wind would be blowing the wrong way down the chimney, when the cottage would be filled with smoke, which so often happened.

I lived in Cornwall for almost nine years, and had my name down on their housing list for seven years because I knew there would come a time when I would have to vacate the cottage, which happened five years later. It was a great wrench when I finally left. I missed living in the country with all the animals around. I could not get any help from the local Housing Authority or anyone else for that matter, even though I had worked for many years in the county, and the last two years doing a lot of voluntary work. So I returned to Devon, and had an assortment of accommodation, at one stage moving three times in one year!

I then applied to a Private Housing Society who let me have a nice newly-built flat to rent, for which I was truly grateful, and have been here almost four years. For the first three years I enjoyed doing Meals-on-Wheels with the WRVS, but then found the steps and stairs were getting too much, especially those three floors up! The lifts were nearly always out of order through vandalism, so reluctantly I had to give that up. These flats are expensive with high rents and rates. So regrettable I have had to part with my car, which had become a luxury item, and I could no longer afford to keep it. Having had one for more than thirty years how I miss it. Especially as I really loved driving. Now shopping has become a real burden. However I must not dwell on these things, but stop and count my numerous blessings.

I have now almost come to the end of my many episodes of past years. As I slow down I am going to enjoy the books in my possession that I never found time to read, and will never feel lonely with all the happy memories stored away to relive again. Perhaps I may have whetted a few people's appetites to get out and about, exploring some of the wonderful places and things that God has given us to enjoy.

Don't wait for humans to accompany you. That's fatal! You will never get anywhere. When travelling days are over you will need those memories of bygone days to fall back on.

One of my lone adventures stands out very clearly before I went to Australia. At that time I was working at Kingston-upon-Hull in East Yorkshire. One day I was looking through a nursing paper and came across an advertisement of a trip to Norway, organised by the Royal College of Nursing — a Seminary which was being held at the Bible College in Oslo. The lectures were being given in English and Norwegian. We were being accommodated at the college. I knew I had worked long enough at Albion Street House to warrant a holiday. It was just a case of getting the right dates, which I did. I had no intentions of going with a group of people, as I knew I would never see all the places I wanted to. So I worked out an itinerary for myself, then lost no time writing to the college and sending my deposit. After receiving confirmation of my booking I was then able to proceed with travel arrangements. I set off ten days before I was due in Oslo, travelling by train from Hull to Newcastle-upon-Tyne, where I boarded a Norwegian boat which left at 4.30 p.m., to cross the North Sea to Stavanger. On the way an excellent buffet meal was provided for passengers, which was luxury plus; the tables loaded with all kinds of fish dishes, a variety of cheeses and salads, and appetising slices of roast beef, the like of which I had not seen in years; crisp bread rolls, and excellent coffee; as much as we liked. When I arrived in Stavanger it was dusk, but time enough to be shown round the airport which had been commandeered by the Germans during the war. I then left on a different boat overnight up the coast to Bergen, arriving at 6.30 a.m., where I had been booked into a very nice hotel on the water's edge, for the next seven days. Bergen is a lovely town and I was able to do a lot of sightseeing by coach to several places of interest.

I had one whole day coach tour out to the Hardanger Fjord, south of Bergen. The scenery was magnificent with the high mountain ranges sheltering the deep water passages beneath. After a very enjoyable week in Bergen I went by express train right across Norway to Oslo. We stopped about half-way at the highest point on the railway for refreshments at the little railway station. The views all round were beautiful, with lots of snow everywhere. On either side of the railway there were fences erected to keep the snow from drifting onto the track. In the valleys were lots of grazing cattle, everywhere looking so clean and peaceful. The train journey was very enjoyable, warm and comfortable.

I arrived at Oslo the day before the course commenced. It was a lovely place to stay. The lectures were held during the mornings, some afternoons and evenings. We had quite a lot of leisure time with the weekend coming in between, so I saw a lot of Oslo and its surroundings. The parks are lovely. One evening some of us went off to a park which had numerous statues lining both sides of the road leading into the park. It was getting dark by the time we got back, but in less than an hour it was broad daylight again. What an experience that was. Now I know what they mean by 'the land of the midnight sun'.

From Oslo I took a different route back, down across country by electric train to Stavanger, which went at great speed, making it almost impossible to take full advantage of the beautiful scenery along the way. Then back across the North Sea to Newcastle and train to Hull. It was a very enjoyable holiday which I shall never forget.

What a blessing I did most of my exploring before I retired. Gone are the days when one could stop the car almost anywhere, and pop into a guest-house for bed and breakfast at one pound a night.

I have travelled by car through every county of England, Ireland, Scotland and Wales, from Land's End to John O'Groats, and had four wonderful holidays in Ireland before the trouble started, each time taking three other friends with me, I being the only driver. In Ireland at that time you could get four gallons of four-star petrol for less than a pound. There was no self-service. The attendant serving would say, 'Have a pound's worth, Miss', which I always did, to oblige. All those friends have since died, but I often think of the happy times we had together, and miss them very much. But that's what life is all about. To my way of thinking, we none of us come into this world, or yet go out, but at what is our right time.

Last year I had my last look at Australia, staying with friends in different parts of the country. I even had a short stay in Christchurch, New Zealand, visiting a friend of over ninety years of age, and seeing all her family who made me most welcome. I must have travelled over 30,000 miles. I did not find travelling as enjoyable as when I went by boat both ways in the nineteen fifties, which was so much more relaxing and less tiring. Those huge jumbo jets are too much for me. There were 421 passengers on the plane I travelled out on, and the queuing to get through Customs was the last straw. It took me weeks to get over it.

But here I am about to complete my story, with the reason why I have had such a satisfying and rewarding life. My Christian life became well rooted in my teens, so with God's help I have never been alone, and have greatly enjoyed my work, from the time I started nursing. Many people will have sung that lovely hymn, 'I've found a friend, oh such a friend'. He loved *me* ere I knew him:

>He drew me with the cords of love,
>And thus He bound me to Him.
>And round my heart still closely twined
>Those ties which nought can sever.
>For I am His, and He is mine.
>Forever, and forever.   And so on:

So wise a *Counsellor* and *Guide*. So mighty a *Defender*. Which I have proved during the wonderful protection afforded me through the war years. I really was in the thick of it, yet I was never really afraid. *The Bible tells us. The fear of man bringeth a snare; but who so putteth his trust in the Lord, shall be safe.* (Proverbs 29. v.25). Sadly that hymn has been left out of the Revised Hymn-book. Over the years it must have been a great help to many people, and definitely for me, setting me off on the right footing.

Now I am going to conclude with the first and last verses of one of my favourite hymns, which sums up what I have been writing about.

(First)   All the way my Saviour leads me.
          What have I to ask beside.
          Can I doubt His tender mercy
          Who through life has been my Guide.
          Heavenly Peace. Divinest comfort.
          Here by Faith with Him to dwell.
          For I know whate'er befalls me,
          Jesus doeth all things well.

(Last)   All the way my Saviour leads me.
          Oh the fullness of His love.
          Perfect rest to me is promised
          In my Father's house above.
          When my spirit clothed immortal
          Wings its flight to realms of day.
          This my song through endless ages,
          Jesus led me all the way.